THE COMMON FOREIGN AND SECURIY POLICY OF THE EUROPEAN UNION

As Implemented in its Overseas Regions, Countries and Territories and its Influence on European Integration

Isaac Freeman

Table of Contents

PREFACE

The research presented to you in this book was mulled in the aftermath of the Arab Spring, when some Middle Eastern guerilla organizations, such as DAESH (a.k.a. ISIS), started to pose a real security threat to the European Union (EU) both internally and externally. Consequently, the union's member states began working closer with each other to encounter this challenge, based on the foundations put forth by the *Treaty of Maastricht* in 1992. The 2016 European Union membership referendum in the United Kingdom (UK), as well as the election of Donald Trump as President of the United States (US) a few months later, created a new political reality for the policy makers in Brussels, regarding foreign policy and security approach.

For more than two decades, the Common Foreign and Security Policy (CFPS), presented in the *Treaty of Maastricht*, was either managed solely by France and the UK or alternatively altogether neglected. As a result, the cohesion approach, attempted by this policy, has utterly failed. In search of a satisfactory explanation to the lack of success in implementing the CFSP, I was looking at what could cause this deficiency. I discovered that by studying the context of the Outermost Regions (OMRs) and the Overseas Countries and Territories (OCTs) of the EU, both the problems and the solutions could be exposed.

The historical background for this research begins with the signing of the *Atlantic Charter* in 1941. This date was chosen as I believe it is an important milestone in the history of European imperialism, where it became clear the pre-war world could not be restored and the enduring empires of European powers must come to an end. From this point on, no more imperial rivalries would dominate politics in the "Old World", but rather they had been replaced with pursue of cooperation, integration and cohesion.

I would like to dedicate a special thanks to Dr. Ayelet Banai and to Dr. Rachel Swissa from the University of Haifa, for helping me conduct this research through their advises and remarks on its initial versions.

Haifa, October 2018

INTRODUCTION

The fall of the Iron Curtain and the dismantling of the Soviet Union (USSR), in the late 1980s and early 1990s, have ended the Cold War and changed the political and strategic reality in Europe and beyond. Into this void, a new inter-governmental organization, the EU, was created by twelve Western European countries. This organization has evolved from the former European Economic Community (EEC), which was established in the 1950s. To this day, it is not clear what the final goal of the union is. Some believe, the current structure is adequate, and only periodic modifications are required from time to time. Others would argue that somewhere in the future, the EU should replace the nation states within the continent, protecting democracy, welfare and minority rights within the union's borders.

In the twenty-five years which have passed since its establishment, the EU had to deal with changing shifts of power in the global political arena. During that time, it became an important player in international diplomacy and economics. After it successfully overcame the 2009 global financial crisis, the EU now faces diplomatic challenges both internal and external. When the results of the EU membership referendum in the UK were revealed on June 2016, and the "Brexit" movement came out triumphant, the EU had to accept the fact one of its most important member states would be leaving the union after due negotiations. In addition to that, on November that same year Donald Trump was elected as President of the US, a turning point in the EU-US relations, especially in regards to their military partnership through NATO.

In light of these developments, the EU has to make evaluation of the threats it is facing, and the capabilities it has to administer them. Hence, the research presented hereinafter, attempts to answer that exact question, by the way of examining the maritime power of the EU in its OMRs and OCTs. But before this subject can be approached, these two terms needs to be further clarified for the reader.

Outermost Regions and Overseas Countries and Territories

According to the *Copenhagen Criteria* – rules which define whether a country is eligible to join the EU – and according to Article 49 of the *Treaty of Maastricht* (a.k.a. the *Treaty on European Union* or *TEU*), any European country which respects the principles of the EU as defined in that treaty, and is located within the boundaries of Europe,[1] may apply to join the union. One might assume, therefore, that the inland borders of the union would not include Brazil, Morocco or Surinam. Yet they do. But how come France, for example, borders Brazil and Surinam – countries which are an entire ocean away from continental Europe? This exceptional reality is due to the EU's outermost regions (OMRs) and overseas countries and territories (OCTs).

At present, there are over thirty regions and territories which belong to EU member states, and have special legal status within the union. They are located across the globe, as remnants of colonial and imperialist eras. While some are only partly members and function with limited autonomy (the OCTs), others are an integral part of their states

---

[1] The classification of a country as "European" is set by the European Commission and the European Council.

and the union (the OMRs), have the Euro as their principal currency, and their citizens have voting rights for European parliament. The different status between these two groups is set by their owner state's foreign policy. More than four-hundred and fifty years of European colonialism around the world, starting in the late fifteenth century, have created special (and different) legal status for both OMRs and OCTs.

Due to their geo-strategic importance – militarily and economically – six of the twenty-eight members of the EU (Denmark, France, the Netherlands, Portugal, Spain and the UK) still possess these territories as national assets, that is to say, they play an important role in the country's politics within the EU and internationally. Located along international trade routes, OMRs and OCTs are considered particularly important on the union's level as well, for they are keeping the EU as a maritime power and maintaining its status as a key player in international politics.

In the days of the EEC, the question of the French overseas departments and territories was considered France's domestic affair. Even after EEC's enlargements in 1973 (Denmark and the UK) and in 1986 (Portugal and Spain), which added several new overseas regions and territories, Brussels preferred to let the new member states governments to deal with their overseas settlements by themselves, thus neglecting these territories until the mid-1990s. Only during the negotiations on the *Treaty of Amsterdam* (1997), Brussels decided to formally differentiate these territories. It introduced the terms Outermost Regions, to define nine regions of three countries (France, Portugal and Spain) which are an integral part of the union, and the Overseas Countries and Territories (OCTs), a group of twenty-five territories of four countries (Denmark, France, the Netherlands and the UK). OCT's inhabitants are EU citizens by the power of the *ius tractum*,[2] yet they do not have voting rights or representation in EU institutions.

Further formalization came about in the *Treaty on the Functioning of the European Union* (TFEU), mostly known as the *Treaty of Lisbon* of 2007, which came into force in 2009. In this treaty, each region and territory was referred to specifically, and its geographic location, topography, population and climate were taken into consideration. This division was made to help EU policy makers adjust the financial aid and political attitude towards each region and territory, according to its needs. In addition to the thirty-four OMRs and OCTs, the EU has some ten other territories with special status within the union. These special cases, like the Spanish cities Ceuta and Melilla in North Africa or the Turkish Republic of Northern Cyprus, are categorized differently and present a unique legal case.

In addition to the EU itself, the TEU introduced also the idea of a Common Foreign and Security Policy (CFSP), an attempt to form a coherent policy for all member states of the EU. While CFSP guidelines were first drafted in 1992, it took almost six years until actual actions were taken in order to make the CFSP effective. In December 1998, Tony Blair, the Prime Minister of the UK and Jacques Chirac the President of France – both leaders of the two most important military powers in Europe – met in a special summit in St. Malo, France. The two countries, reluctant to allow the EU to influence their defence and security policies, became leading voices of the EU's foreign policy and

---

[2] *Ius tractum* is a legal term commonly used in international law, which refers to the right to expand treaties implementation in special cases. In the case of the EU, as all citizens of a member state are EU citizens as well, people who live in the OCTs are thus EU citizens.

defence policy overseas. Moreover, Britain and France shaped the CFSP throughout the years and left Germany, the most populated and economically strongest member of the EU, without any decisive influence on major policy developments.

Case studies

I chose to two case studies in order to explore the implementation of the CFSP overseas. The French island of La Réunion, located in the Indian Ocean about 175 km eastwards to Madagascar, will be used as a case study for the OMRs, and the British Falkland Islands, located in the Atlantic Ocean some 600 km eastwards to Argentina (who also claims the ownership of the islands), will be used as a case study for the OCTs. La Réunion uniqueness is by being the only region of the EU (in Europe and beyond) which is also a member of another political organization – the Indian Ocean Commission (IOC). Using this case study shows how the EU reinforces its foreign policy in the overseas. The Falkland Islands, which hold the largest military base of the EU outside Europe, is as an example to the EU's overseas security approach. The Falkland War of 1982 presented a dilemma to European policymakers, as part of the EU was attacked by a non-EU force. While French regions are part of the union (as it is an OMR), the UK keeps its territories out of the union.

Current literature provides only few insights on OMRs' and OCTs' implication on CFSP. Even scholars admit that it is not an easy task to find resources dealing with the OMRs or OCTs in light of the CFSP. Paul Nielsen, a former member of the European Commissioner for Development, wrote in a review on a book dealing with the OMRs and

OCTs that is has "information deficit on the subject". This remark by Nielsen emphasizes how much the question of the OMRs and OCTs, especially as art of the CFSP, has been generally neglected by scholars. In the following pages, I will also explain what the comprehensive approach of the EU is. This approach was defined by the European Commission as "a common and shared responsibility of all EU actors in Brussels, in Member States and on the ground in third countries".

The decision to analyze only two case studies is strongly influenced by the type of political phenomena under study, and how they are conceptualized. Alternatively, some analysts believe that political phenomena are best understood through the careful examination of a small number of cases. Cases should also be selected to provide the kind of control and variation required by the research problem. This requires that the universe or subclass of events be clearly defined so that appropriate case can be selected.

Since the research itself was first presented in 2017, and as the UK is still officially a member of the EU, I decided to keep the Falklands as a case study, since they are used to explain the general idea of the CFSP in the OCTs, and other islands could have been chosen instead, with the same conclusion still being applied.

The few books which deal with the OMRs and the OCTs, analyze them from the judicial aspect, since all except one (French Guiana) are islands, and have a special legal status according to maritime law. The examination of the elements of security and defence and of foreign affairs is almost completely neglected. The reason of choosing the examination of the larger scale CFSP is that some territories do not contribute much to the military power of the EU, yet their value to the foreign policy of the EU is great.

Since 1992 the union treated OMRs as an asset for its increased involvement in regional development overseas. Until that year, the OMRs were subjected solely to their "parent state", and thus the EU did not gain much as a global actor overseas. Therefore the Falkland War of 1982 could be considered as a matter of the UK alone, and not of the European Community (EC). Nowadays, however, with the attempts to increase the European integration among its member states, the EU tries to make it clearer that a war in a remote region or post of one of the EU member states is a matter of the EU, or at least should be – according to the CFSP.

Diplomacy and security are dealt with scarcely, and receive only a marginal role in academic research. Thus, the current research offers to present how the EU uses its OMRs and OCTs in order to strengthen its overseas foreign policy, its maritime security policy and its interstate integration.

CHAPTER ONE

The Creation of the Overseas Territories

In order to understand the special status of the OMRs and OCTs within the EU, one must first understand the process of disbanding the overseas colonies of some European countries after the Second World War. These colonies came to be in a long process, starting at the sixteenth century, which reached its peak in the second half of the nineteenth century. This episode in European history is known as the *Age of Colonialism*, and thus the counter action to colonialism is known as decolonization. This chapter will deal with the historical changes at the European overseas colonies since 1941 to this day and will focus mainly on France and the UK.

On August 14, 1941, Winston Churchill, the Prime Minister of the UK and Franklin D. Roosevelt, the US President, signed the *Atlantic Charter* in Placentia Bay, Newfoundland, Canada. Despite being signed almost four months before the US had joined the war, the charter already organized the new world order, after the defeat of Nazi Germany. The final statement of the charter consists of eight principles:

1. The US and the UK seek no aggrandizement, territorial or other.

2. They desire to see no territorial changes that do not accord with the freely expressed wishes of the peoples concerned.

3. They respect the right of all peoples to choose the form of Government under which they will live.

4. Trade barriers were to be lowered.

5. There was desire to bring about a global economic cooperation and advancement of social welfare.

6. The participants saw to establish a peace which will afford to all nations the means of dwelling in safety within their own boundaries, and work for a world all the men in all the lands would be free of want and fear.

7. The participants would work for freedom of the seas and oceans.

8. They believed that in order to establish a wider and permanent system of general security, there was to be disarmament of aggressor nations, and a post-war common disarmament.

Shortly after signing the charter, on September 24, 1941, other Allied nations had endorsed it. Amongst the ratifying states were the governments in exile of Belgium, Czechoslovakia, Greece, Luxembourg, the Netherlands, Norway, Poland, and Yugoslavia, and even the USSR. The charter also presented the basic principles to be used by an organization which would be created after the war – the United Nations (UN) – whose establishment was declared by twenty-six governments, on January 1, 1942, in Washington DC.

The broadly shared American vision among government officials was that the *Atlantic Charter* meant the end of the *Imperial Era*, and the dismantling of all European colonial empires, including the British. But Churchill refused to discuss the future of the British Empire with Roosevelt during their talks. Moreover, as far as the British were concerned, Article 3 of the Atlantic Charter, which states that: *"They* (the US and the UK) *respect the right of all peoples to choose the form of Government under which they will live; and they wish to see sovereign rights and self-government restored to those who have been forcibly deprived of them"*, did not apply to the nations living under the rule of their Empire. The American Under-Secretary of State, Sumner Welles, replied to these claims by the British in 1942: "*If this war is in fact a war for the liberation of peoples, it must assure the sovereign equality of peoples throughout the world, as well as in the world of the Americas. Our victory must bring in its train the liberation of all peoples. Discrimination between peoples because of their race, creed, or color must be abolished. The age of imperialism is ended.*"

Eventually, the British had no choice but to accept the American view of the charter, since it was the US who provided the resources for the Allies to win the war. The Americans were aiming to weaken the European powers, in order to gain more power themselves, but the British and French, despite eventually giving up on most of their colonies, were not willing to give up so easily, and without literally fighting back.

Decolonization after the Second World War

The disassembling of European overseas colonies was initiated already after the First World War and continued during the Second World War; but the process was accelerated especially in the years 1945–1965. The immense devastation in Europe after the war required the reconstruction of the entire continent like never before. As a result, Former European powers gave up most of their overseas colonies. The overseas colonies thus lost their status as national assets, and some, like India for the UK, became a heavy financial burden. In addition to the *Atlantic Charter*, some nations in Southeast Asia, who suffered from the Japanese occupation and colonial extortion during the war, were promised to become independent in exchange to their cooperation in the war effort alongside the Allies. Colonized nations of Southeast Asia were to gain independence from their European rulers, as much as from their Japanese conquerors, once the war was over. But neither the British nor the French intend to go as far as to offer full liberation in the form of independence to their colonies in Asia or the Pacific.

Nevertheless, in 1947, the British decided to leave the British Raj,[3] which consequently gained India its independence some months later. A partition between India and Pakistan soon followed. In 1948, the UK granted independence to Burma and Ceylon and in 1957 to Malaya. The last country to gain its independence from the British in this wave of decolonization was Singapore (1963). France also had to cope with demands for independence from its colonies: In 1946 it became embroiled in a colonial war in Indochina,[4] which ended in 1953 with the victory of the Việt Minh[5] over the French forces, which were obliged to leave the country. Laos and Cambodia also gained their independence due to the French departure. What the European empires did not fully understand was that once Indonesians, Chinese, Burmese, Indians and other nations had seen how a fellow Asian nation (Japan) humiliates European colonial powers – the notion of Western omnipotence in East Asia was due to an end. Thus, within eighteen years, all European colonies in Southeast Asia, except the Portuguese possessions of Goa and Timor, became independent states.

The failure to keep their overseas colonies in Asia did not mean that France or the UK were willing to give up their colonial empires in

---

[3] The British Raj was the rule of Britain the Indian subcontinent since 1858.
[4] Indochina, or the Indochinese Peninsula, is a historical name that refers to the continental portion of Southeast Asia, lying east of India and roughly south or southwest of China.
[5] Vietnamese for: *League for Independence of Vietnam.*

Africa as well. Both countries reacted to threats and losses in Asia by looking more to Africa. They showed no interest in relinquishing their colonies there, since they viewed Africa as giving them equal status with the new Super Powers: the US and the USSR. Thus, they were ignoring for a longer while (until the mid-1960s) their actual political power in the post-war world international system. The French government chose to inflict collective terror against categories of people among whom rebels were supposed to lurk. At the same time, during the repression of the revolt in Madagascar in 1947 and the Algerian War of 1954–1962, as well as the Vietnam War up to the French defeat in 1954, the French government also tried to get the locals to see the benefits of inclusion in the French policy. The UK's policy was different. It fostered hope among Africans, that in the future – some colonies could reach the same level of independence Canada had at that time: a self-governing dominion.

These differences between British and French attitude towards Africa is based on their differences in foreign policy approaches. While France traditionally leaned more on diplomacy and spheres of influence approach, the UK preferred the commonwealth approach and emphasized military strength and economic connections with their dominions. Thus, the French were looking forward to more cooperation with their government in Paris, while the British accepted loosen control over the dominions, as long as it did not contradict British interests.

Suez Crisis

The British and French were unwilling to give up neither their colonies in Africa nor what they conceived as a national asset – like the

Suez Canal.[6] The canal was so strategically important, that both states were willing to send a third party (Israel) to fight a former British colony (Egypt) in order to keep it under their control. After the Egyptian president, Gamal Abdel Nasser, nationalized the canal in 1956, Anthony Eden, the Prime Minister of the UK, was under immense domestic pressure to return the canal to British control: its loss threatened British economic and military interests in the Middle East. British press severely condemned the nationalization and *The Times* compared Nasser's "coup" with Hitler's reoccupation of the Rhineland in 1936. The French Prime Minister, Guy Mollet, was outraged by Nasser's move, and demanded him to withdraw his forces. French public opinion supported Mollet, and apart from the Communists, all of the criticism of his government came from the right, who very publicly doubted that a socialist like Mollet had the guts to go to war with Nasser.

In August 1956, British and French military strategists began to plan an invasion. The plan was that Israel would initiate a first strike, to allow free passage to its ships, while the British and the French would intervene to restore peace. On October 29, Israel's army attacked and made rapid progress. On October 30, France and the UK issued their ultimatums, which Egypt rejected, ordering a full mobilization and announcing that they would refer the matter to the UN's Security Council (UNSC). Anglo-French air attacks began at midnight on October 30. On November 2 the UN passed a resolution calling for an immediate ceasefire, but Britain, together with France who had no forces ashore, continued their air operations.

---

[6] The Universal Suez Ship Canal Company (French: *Compagnie universelle du canal maritime de Suez*) was the corporation that constructed and operated the Suez Canal, and was at that time in the hands of British and French businessmen.

Eventually, it was American pressure which had forced Eden and Mollet to ceasefire. Nasser remained firmly in power; the Canal was blocked; Britain's and France's relations with their allies were in disarray and their prestige and moral standing were badly damaged. The Suez Crisis may have been a milestone in ending of the British and French empires, but it was not its starting point. The age of imperialism ended in the Second World War, with the signing of the Atlantic Charter. After Suez, the idea of empire, in both Britain and France, remained entrenched only in some politicians' minds.

The Evolution of the Overseas Territories

Although the roots of the EU can be found in the establishment of the European Coal and Steel Community (ECSC) by the *Treaty of Paris* of 1951, the attitude of the EEC towards its member states' overseas regions and territories was decided during the negotiations of the *Treaty of Rome*. Article 227 of the latter dealt with the overseas regions of the EEC members. According to this Article, the overseas regions of the EEC member states were to be part of the EEC, while the overseas territories were not. France's overseas settlements are divided into two categories: overseas departments (French: départments d'outre-mer or DOMs) and overseas territories (French: territories d'outre-mer or TOMs). The TOMs are similar to the British dominions, as they are semi-independent political entities. The DOMs, however, are part of France in all aspects.[7] Thus, French Guiana, a French DOMs, was to be part of the EEC, and nowadays it is part of the EU, yet Suriname, which

---

[7] The French Republic is divided into eighteen regions (or departments): thirteen in the mainland France and five (Guadeloupe, French Guiana, Martinique, Mayotte and La Réunion) overseas.

was at that time an overseas territory of the Netherlands, was never a part of the EEC, and in 1975 it gained its independence from the Dutch.

But even on the state-level, the status of the OMRs was unclear during the 1950s. When an Israeli delegation, led by Shimon Peres,[8] offered in 1959 to lease French Guiana from France, Jacques Soustelle, the French Minister of the Colonies at that time, agreed to the deal. As far as the French was concerned, this territory was empty and remote, and no specific duty was set for the region. Eventually, the Israeli parliament rejected the idea for internal reasons, and sixteen years would pass before French Guiana's full potential is discovered,[9] before it became the center of the European Space Agency (ESA). Furthermore, the French, who had plenty of colonies in Africa before the 1960s, offered to create a common European-African market, which would benefit all sides (but mostly Europe). Africa's independence ambition won, and the French idea was shortly rejected.

When Denmark, Ireland and the UK joined the EEC in 1973, it was assumed other overseas territories could become overseas regions of the EEC, but only Greenland and Gibraltar were interested in joining this small group. Eventually, both lost their status as overseas regions; Greenland left the EEC in 1985, and Gibraltar, although remained in the community, was no longer an overseas region, after Spain's accession to the community in 1986. Greenland's decision to leave the EEC followed another Danish territory – the Faroe Islands – who decided not to join the community in the first place. Their reasoning, which influenced

---

[8] Shimon Peres was a leading figure of the Israeli foreign affairs for many years. Among his political positions through the years he was minister of foreign affairs of Israel and president of Israel (2007–2014).

[9] Guiana Space Centre (French: *Centre spatial guyanais*) is located at 5°14′14″N 52°45′38″W, which makes it the closest launch site to the equator in the world.

Greenland's decision to leave, was the fear of the Faroese they would be left out of jobs if big companies from mainland Europe could fish next to their islands. The British territory Bermuda is another example of an overseas region of the EEC which downgraded itself to a level of a territory. Just like Greenland, the government of Bermuda did not want the EEC territorial committees who sit in Brussels, almost 6,000 km away, would decide their economic agenda, since the conditions of an island in the middle of the ocean are not the same as a continental region in the heart of Europe.

The OMRs and OCTs Following the Treaties of Amsterdam and Lisbon

Unlike the case of the *Treaty of Rome*, in the TEU there was no reference to the overseas territories of the EU member states. It was only five years later, in the *Treaty of Amsterdam*, that the overseas territories would be mentioned again in an important EU treaty, and for the first time – be examined not only on a state-level, but also on the EU-level. Article 229 of the *Treaty of Amsterdam*, recognized for the first time, a group of regions which would be referred to from this treaty onwards as "Outermost Regions". But even in this treaty, the reference was made only to those territories which were considered as part of their "parent states", and thus – part of the EU. Territories which were (and still are) partly autonomous, had to wait for the TFEU, a decade later, in order to be fully addressed by the EU.

The *Treaty on the Functioning of the European Union* (TFEU) is currently the last major treaty concerning the functioning of the EU. The treaty was signed in Lisbon, Portugal in 2007, and was enacted in January 2009. This treaty amends some aspects of the EU functioning in general, but it also specifically addressed the non-EU overseas territories. The treaty forms a clear distinction between the OMRs and the OCTs, and defines each and every one of them. It also defines who is responsible to each group: OMRs are under the jurisdiction of the EU, whereas OCTs are under the jurisdiction of the member states.

The treaty announces the OMRs would receive financial aid to promote the economic development of areas where the standard of living is abnormally low or where there is serious underemployment. The OMRs are also promised to receive aid to promote the execution of an important project of common European interest or to remedy a serious disturbance in the economy of a member state. The treaty also sets the ground to future "upgrade" of an OCTs to an OMRs, and according to Article 335 (6), the European Council may, on the initiative of the member state concerned, adopt a decision amending the status, with regard to the union, of a Danish, French or Netherlands country or territory. The European Council shall act unanimously after consulting the Commission. But besides the economic development of its OMRs, the EU sets itself a goal in this treaty, of having a coherent policy towards the OMRs. Article 174 of that treaty declares: "In order to promote its overall harmonious development, the union shall develop and pursue its actions leading to the strengthening of its economic, social and territorial cohesion. In particular, the union shall aim at reducing disparities between the levels of development of the various regions and the backwardness of the least favored regions."

Looking forward into the future, the OMRs and OCTs are now included in the long-term agendas of the EU. One of these agendas is the *Territorial Agenda of the European Union 2020* (TA2020),[10] an official paper of the EU, which presents spatial planning for territorial development. This agenda is under the responsibility of the ministers for Spatial Planning and Territorial Development, the European Commission and the Committee of the Regions. The TA2020 is an action oriented policy framework, created to support territorial cohesion in Europe as a new goal of the EU, as introduced by the TFEU. The Agenda outlines objectives in accordance with the time horizon of major policy documents until 2020. The ministers, who oversee the execution of Agenda, consider the integration of territories through territorial cooperation to be an important factor in fostering global competitiveness. In this way, potentials such as valuable natural, landscape and cultural heritage, city networks and labor markets divided by borders can be better utilized. Special attention shall be paid to areas along external borders of the EU in this regard (e.g. Brazil, Suriname etc.).

Territorial integration and cooperation can create a critical mass for development, diminishing economic, social and ecological fragmentation, building mutual trust and social capital. Cross border and transnational functional regions may require proper policy coordination between different countries. The agenda supports transnational and cross border integration of regions going beyond cooperation projects and focusing on developments and results of real cross-border or transnational relevance. According to it, European Territorial Cooperation should be better embedded within national, regional and local development strategies. The economic competitiveness can be

---

[10] The *Territorial Agenda of the European Union 2020* is an action oriented policy, which sets the goals of development of the EU overseas regions and territories until 2020

enhanced by the development of globally integrated economic sectors and strong local economies. The use of social capital, territorial assets, and the development of innovation and smart specialization strategies in a place-based approach can play a key role.

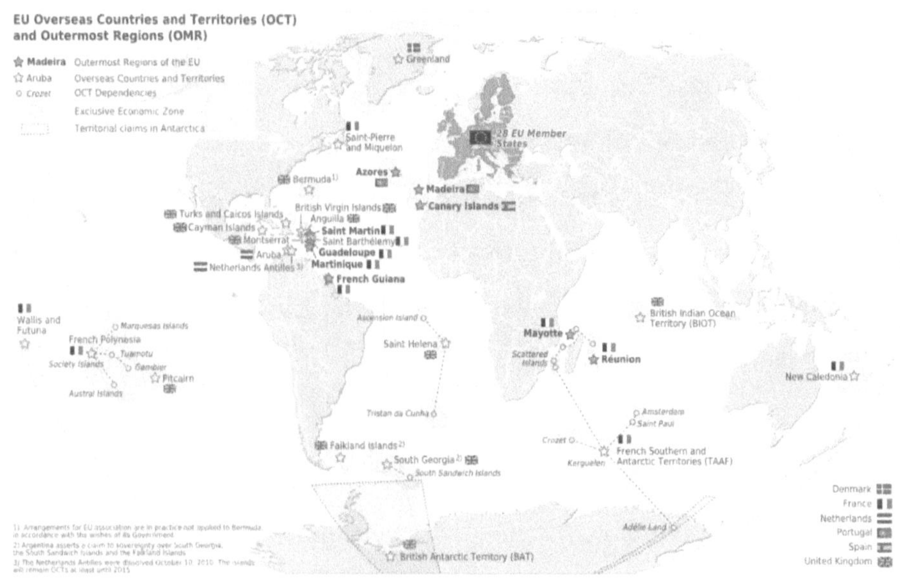

The OMRs and OCTs, as of 2007

Furthermore, integration of local endowments, characteristics and traditions into the global economy is important in strengthening local responses and reducing vulnerability to external forces. Improving local economies through development of local products and markets, business environments and building up cohesive and strong local communities can be effective tools for the EU to increase its influence on its OMRs neighbors. Consideration of territorial impacts and the territorial coordination of policies are particularly important at national and regional levels. This coordination should be supported by territorially sensitive evaluation and monitoring practices, further strengthening the contribution of territorial analysis to impact assessments. These territorial aspects could be integrated into regular national and EU reports and evaluations related to Cohesion Policy[11] and *Europe 2020 Strategy*,[12] avoiding unnecessary bureaucracy.

Chapter Summary

For centuries European kingdoms and states established and maintained overseas colonies in all continents around the globe. The process of dismantling the colonial empires which arose as a result of this colonization, began in the nineteenth century, but was accelerated after the Second World War. Nevertheless, six European countries kept some of these territories, which are placed in strategic locations, as national assets, either as integral part of their countries or as semi-independent political entities. These territories have special status within the EU, and this status have changed since the first reference towards them in the Treaty of Rome, and until the specific articles dedicated to them in the TFEU. The main reason for the drastic change in EU's attitude towards its OMRs is the political structure of the EU in the mid-1990s, comparing to 1957. The EEC had less authority than the EU, and in the first years, there was only one country with overseas regions (France). Thus, the EEC leaders referred to the subject of these regions as a French matter. Nowadays, there are more countries with overseas regions, and since the 1970s, the French have pushed towards "Europazation" of the OMRs, as they believed it would benefit the EEC,

---

[11] The "Cohesion policy" is the policy behind the various projects all over Europe, which receive funding from the European Regional Development Fund (ERDF), the European Social Fund (ESF) and the Cohesion Fund.

[12] Europe 2020 is a 10-year strategy proposed by the European Commission in 2010 for advancement of the economy of the EU.

but even further – it could upgrade France's prestige within the EEC and among the international community.

The country who mostly pushed forward the subject was France. The French foreign policy is based on the theory of spheres of influence, and thus the French use their DOM in order to gain diplomatic influence in the neighboring countries near their overseas departments. In contrast, stands the UK, whose foreign policy promotes the commonwealth approach and emphasizes military strength, and that is the reason why most of their dominions are somewhat autonomous. Unlike the French, the British do not want their overseas policies to be dominated from Brussels, and the results of the 2016 "Brexit" referendum constitutes as evidence that the British rather leave the EU permanently, than to let someone who is not British to dictate their foreign policy.

CHAPTER TWO

The EU's Foreign Policy

The EU's CFSP is divided in two: a common foreign policy and a common security policy. Though both policies are aimed to manage the relations between the EU and "the rest of the world", each has its own characteristics, methods and goals. Diplomacy, or foreign policy, is part of the "soft power" tools of the EU, which are used to gain political achievements without the use of violent force. These tools can be in a form of Non-Governmental Organizations (NGOs), volunteering to promote a certain feature in a non-EU society; a trade agreement which aims to promote consumption of commodity manufactured in the EU member states; even an easier visa policy towards a certain country or region, which would allow its citizens easier travel into and within EU and its territories can be considered as a "soft power" instrument.

An example for such is the European Neighbourhood Policy (ENP), which seeks to establish foreign relations with countries to the east and south of the EU.[13] Through the ENP, the EU works with its southern and eastern neighbors to achieve the closest possible political association and the greatest possible degree of economic integration, thus gaining political influence over these countries. This goal builds on common interests and on values – democracy, the rule of law, respect for human rights and social cohesion. The ENP is a key part of the EU's foreign policy in Eastern Europe, Northern Africa and the Middle East. The ENP is primarily an attempt to create good neighbors: namely, the

---

[13] These countries are: Algeria, Armenia, Azerbaijan, Belarus, Egypt, Georgia, Israel, Jordan, Lebanon, Libya, Morocco, Moldova, the Palestinian Authority, Syria, Tunisia and Ukraine.

kind who conforms not only to "EU values" generally speaking, but also to EU standards and laws in specific economic and social areas.

This chapter will present the actual foreign policy of the EU implemented in its overseas regions through a case study of one OMR: the French DOM La Réunion. Through this example, I will examine if and how it complies with the EU's CFSP and the EU treaties. Choosing the island of La Réunion out of the other eight possible options was due to the following reasons:

1. It is the largest OMR of the EU in the Indian Ocean (in terms of geographical area, population and GDP), and it is a gate for the EU to countries located in East Africa, Southern Arabia and South Asia. Politically, it is considered as part of the Indian Ocean region, which consists of South Africa, Republic of Angola, Botswana, the Comoros, India, Madagascar, Mauritius, Namibia, Seychelles, Zimbabwe and Zambia

2. It is a member of the *Indian Ocean Commission* (IOC; French: *Commission de l'Océan Indien* or COI) – an intergovernmental organization founded in 1982 which composed, in addition to La Réunion, of four other former colonies of France in the African Indian Ocean: Comoros, Madagascar, Mauritius and Seychelles. The main objectives of the IOC are: diplomatic cooperation; economic and commercial cooperation; cooperation in the field of agriculture, maritime fishing, and the conservation of resources and ecosystems; and cooperation in cultural, scientific, technical, educational and judicial fields.

3. It is the second most populated OMR (after the Spanish Canary Islands), yet France's political importance within the EU is greater than

Spain's. Moreover, La Réunion's location of in a more politically strategic location in comparison to the Canary Islands was another decisive factor.

4. Since I am capable of reading in French, yet neither Portuguese nor Spanish, a DOM of France was a preferable choice as a case study for this research. Nevertheless, researchers who seek to examine other factors of the EU's CFSP might have chosen a different case study.

5. Militarily, La Réunion is considered as a Forward Presence Base of the EU,[14] and thus it has also military strategic importance in keeping the EU a maritime power.

French Presence in La Réunion

La Réunion is located in the Indian Ocean, approximately 800 km east of Madagascar and about 200 km west of Mauritius, and its administrative capital (French: *préfecture*), Saint-Denis, is located some 9,400 km from the French capital – Paris. Its total area is 2,512 km^2 and it has approximately 850,000 inhabitants. The first European discovery of the uninhabited island was around 1507 by the Portuguese explorer Diego Fernandes Pereira[15] and not much is known of the island's history prior to that era. The island remained uninhabited until 1665 when French settlers sent by a public commercial enterprise called *Compagnie française pour le commerce des Indes orientales*[16] colonized the island, and named it Île Bourbon in honor of the French royal house of

---

[14] The term will be fully explained in chapter 3.

[15] Diego Fernandes Pereira was a Portuguese navigator who lived during the sixteenth century. Not much is known about his life, including his year of birth or his year of death.

[16] *Compagnie française pour le commerce des Indes orientales* was a public commercial enterprise, founded in France in 1664, and its aim was to compete with the British and Dutch East India companies in the East Indies.

Bourbon. On March 23, 1793, two months and two days after the execution of the former king of France, Louis Capet (a.k.a. Louis XVI), the French National Convention (French: *Convention nationale*) decided the island's name it too much attached with the *Ancien Régime* (i.e. the monarchy) and decided to rename it Île de la Réunion, in honor to the meeting (La Réunion in French) between the Paris Commune and the revolutionary fédérés from Marseilles in the insurrection of August 10, 1792[17] at the Palais des Tuileries.

Although located more than 8,500 km from the southernmost tips of France, the political turmoil of the French Republic did not bypass the island of La Réunion. For forty-five years the island changed its name three times, each time according to the identity of the ruler of France. In 1801, the island was renamed Île Bonaparte, after France's First Consul Napoleon Bonaparte. As part of the Napoleonic Wars, the island was invaded in 1810 by a joint effort of a French Royal Navy squadron (who used the old name Île Bourbon) and British reinforcement. When the island was restored to France by the Congress of Vienna[18] in 1815, it retained the name of "Bourbon" until the French Revolution of 1848, when the island was named once again "Île de la Réunion".

Traditionally, the economy of La Réunion was based on agriculture, and from the nineteenth century, for a period of about a century long, the primary crop grown on the island was sugarcanes.

---

[17] The insurrection of August 10, 1792, was the capture of the French Royal family in Paris, which resulted in the fall of the French monarchy.

[18] The Congress of Vienna was a conference of ambassadors of European states, held in Vienna from 1814 to 1815. The objective of the Congress was to provide a long-term peace plan for Europe by settling critical issues arising from the French Revolutionary Wars and the Napoleonic Wars.

Slavery and slave trade in (and to) the island were abolished in 1794, as part of the French Revolution reforms, but it was reintroduction by Napoleon in 1802 and continued until the 1810 invasion of the royalists and the British, and the slave trade brought to an end by the British once the island was under the royalists' control again. Slavery itself, however, remained a legal custom until 1835, when it was formally and finally abolished. The First World War skipped La Réunion without any significant events, but the Second World War was slightly different. The island was under the authority of Vichy France since July 1940, until it was re-occupied by the Allies in an invasion performed by the French destroyer *Léopard* of the *Forces navales française libres* on November 28, 1942.

Since the first colonization of La Réunion by the French in the seventeenth century, it was considered a dependency[19] of France. Only in 1946 did it receive a status of a DOM, alongside with French Guiana, Guadeloupe and Martinique. The main reason France decided to grant these four colonies a status of overseas departments, rather than granting them more political autonomy, was that France's policy in the question of the overseas colonies was towards assimilation, not separation. This principle was set already in the French Revolution of 1789, when the revolutionists believed the ideas of the revolution should be universal, and granted to every man and woman under French rule, including in its overseas colonies. For seventeen years since La Réunion had become a DOM, there were some attempts to push towards full independence from France. These attempts were led by the communist party of La

---

[19] According to the United Nations General Assembly Resolution 1514 (from 1960), a dependency is a territory that does not possess full political independence or sovereignty as a sovereign state, yet remains politically outside of the controlling state's integral area.

Réunion – *La parti communiste Réunionnais* (PCR) – but eventually the French government under Charles de Gaulle managed to help its preferable candidate to win the 1963 elections, and the idea of independence was abandoned.

La Réunion and the EU

Like all other OMRs, La Réunion was neglected by the EU policy makers until 1997, and all its political affairs were engaged only by the French government, as it is an administrative department of France. But as it was explained in the previous chapter, it was not until 2007, when the TFEU was signed, that the OMRs received full attention from Brussels. The main rule governing OMRs status in EU law is the goal of the full incorporation of these territories within the scope *ratione materiae*[20] of EU law, while taking into account the natural specificity of these regions. This clearly follows from Article 355(1) TFEU, establishing that "the provisions of the Treaties shall apply to Guadeloupe, French Guiana, Martinique, Réunion, Saint-Barthélemy, Saint-Martin, the Azores, Madeira and the Canary Islands in accordance with Article 349 [TFEU]," the latter requiring the Council to "adopt specific measures aimed, in particular, at laying down the conditions of application of the Treaties to those regions."

Historically, the development of the OMRs' status has been marked by a constant shift in the balance between the ideal of full incorporation of these regions into the scope of the *acquis*[21] and the need

---

[20] *Jurisdiction Ratione Materiae* is a Latin term which refers to the court's authority to decide a particular case.
[21] The Community acquis (French: *acquis communautaire*) is the accumulated legislation, legal acts, and court decisions which constitute the body of EU law.

to pay adequate attention to the objective differentiating factors able to influence the application of the law in those regions, putting them in a position different from that of the European territories of the member states. In the past decade the EU Commission gradually recognized the importance of certain overseas territories of its member states, and therefore there has been extended initiatives launched and considerable activities accelerated in certain policies. This process had begun in the end of the first decade of the twenty-first century, along with increasing attention to remote lands adjacent to countries which are currently seeking possibilities to set up new political and economic relations with the EU itself or with any EU member state. An example to this change of attitude of the EU towards some of its overseas territories can be seen in Article 349 TFEU, which states the following:

"Taking account of the structural social and economic situation of Guadeloupe, French Guiana, Martinique, Réunion, Saint-Barthélemy, Saint-Martin, the Azores, Madeira and the Canary Islands, which is compounded by their remoteness, insularity, small size, difficult topography and climate, economic dependence on a few products, the permanence and combination of which severely restrain their development, the Council, on a proposal from the Commission and after consulting the European Parliament, shall adopt specific measures aimed, in particular, at laying down the conditions of application of the Treaties to those regions, including common policies". These measures "concern in particular areas such as customs and trade policies, fiscal policy, free zones, agriculture and fisheries policies, conditions for supply of raw materials and essential consumer goods, State aids and conditions of access to structural funds and to horizontal Union programs". They shall be adopted "without undermining the integrity and the coherence of the Union legal order, including the internal market and common policies".

In this treaty, the OMRs of the EU have well-defined specifications from which the most determinates are the remoteness, insularity and relatively small sized territory with difficult topography and climate. Due to these factors, the OMRs have economic dependence on a small number of products and services. However, these regions also have major assets and the potential not only to contribute to their own development, but also to that of the EU as a whole. They can act as excellent laboratories for studying and combating the effects of climate change, they have exceptional biodiversity and marine ecosystems, great potential for the development of renewable energies and leading-edge agri-environmental research, and so on.

In the Indian Ocean region only the island of La Réunion represents EU interests as being an OMR.[22] La Réunion is also an "active border" of the EU. Aware of its assets from its double membership (the EU and the Indian Ocean region), La Réunion intends to use regional cooperation in a strategy of development in partnership. The Regional Council of La Réunion has also initiated a series of partnerships with regional territories. These territories include the IOC, Eastern Africa (the South African Province of Kwazulu-Natal, Mozambique and Zimbabwe) and Asia (Vietnam, the Indian State of Karnataka and the Chinese Province of Tianjin). At the heart of the

---

[22] Mayotte, the other DOM of France which is categorized as an OMR, which is located approximately 1,500 km north-west to La Réunion, and about 30 km north-west to Madagascar, is the smallest (in geographic area and population) and the poorest of all OMRs, and thus is not taken into account by scholars as representing EU interests in the Indian Ocean region.

Indian Ocean, the island also enjoys the status as an OMR. Many competitive advantages are induced: access to a market of five-hundred million European consumers; belonging to the free trade zone of France and South Africa; a label of European manufacturing; political stability and jurisdiction; a guarantee of monetary stability that reinforces by the introduction of the Euro.

Cohesion policy is a key tool for the OMRs' regional development strategies. It provides important support for convergence towards the *Europe 2020* objectives and for modernizing and diversifying the regions' economies. The European Regional Development Fund (ERDF), which includes an additional grant for the OMRs to offset the extra costs they incur, the Cohesion Fund (for the Portuguese OMRs) and the European Social Fund (ESF) are major tools that contribute to structuring public and private investment in these regions. The OMRs are also beneficiaries of various financial instruments and special schemes that have been introduced in the areas of fisheries (through the European Fisheries Fund – EFF) and agricultural development (with the help of the European Agricultural Fund for Rural Development – EAFRD and the Program of Options Specifically Relating to Remoteness and Insularity – POSEI). The OMRs are closely involved in the ERDF co-financed Territorial Cooperation Programs, which act as a vital tool for strengthening their regional integration. There were four transnational and cross-border cooperation programs devoted to them for the period 2007-13:

1. The "MAC" program, involving Madeira, the Azores and the Canary Islands and also covering neighboring west African countries;

2. The "INTERREG – Caribbean" program linking Martinique, Guadeloupe, Saint Martin and French Guiana and also involving the other Caribbean states;

3. The "Indian Ocean" program, involving La Réunion and its neighboring states in the Indian Ocean;

4. The "Amazonia" program involving French Guiana, Surinam and north-eastern Brazil's Amazonian states (Amapà, Parà and Amazonas).

EU Projects in La Réunion

As the subject for a case study in this chapter is the French OMR La Réunion, an example of some EU projects in the island will now be presented in more detail, in order to fully understand how the EU involvement in regional development.

Remote Sensing Station for Satellite-Assisted Environmental Monitoring (SEAS-OI)

As in all island territories, the management of space and regional planning are crucially important in the face of demographic growth, agricultural development, urbanization, natural disasters, etc. Satellite observation and monitoring have become vital tools in helping decision-making and in the daily management of land and ocean territories. It is against this background that the La Réunion region has undertaken the construction of a satellite image receiving and processing station. The project was funded by the ERDF, in a total sum of €10,190,000, and it was operating in the years 2008–2014. SEAS-OI aimed to put in place a center of excellence in remote sensing using a station to receive and process high-resolution satellite images covering the entire south-west area of the Indian Ocean. Two types of image need to be processed: radar images (RADARSAT-2[23] and ENVISAT[24]) and optical images (SPOT-4[25] and SPOT-5). Radar images are particularly well suited to the monitoring of maritime areas.

Optical images offer resolutions that can be accurate to 2.5 meters and which make many applications in terms of land imaging and mapping possible. These will be useful in relation to regional problems concerning land planning, the management of natural land environments, maritime monitoring, epidemiological monitoring, the preservation of biodiversity, monitoring of climate indicators and the management of natural hazards. The SEAS-OI program gathered several objectives: provide a "real-time" access to satellite data; provide operational solutions to public institutions (decision-making support); improve methodologies in the field of remote sensing and image analysis; develop regional cooperation through scientific and operational projects in remote sensing; transfer competences to the countries of the COI. SEAS-OI was the pole of remote sensing of the Indian Ocean, involving a large number of partners from France and its region of interest. It offered free access to original SAR[26] RADARSAT-2 data to public and scientific communities, and it gathered expertise in remote sensing to carry out innovative scientific and operational projects.

---

[23] RADARSAT-2 is an Earth observation satellite of the Canadian Space Agency that was launched in 2007.

[24] ENVISAT ("Environmental Satellite") was a large Earth-observing satellite, whose mission ended in. It was operated by the European Space Agency (ESA).

[25] SPOT (French for: *Satellite Pour l'Observation de la Terre*) is a commercial high-resolution optical imaging Earth observation satellite system operating from space.

[26] A Synthetic Aperture Radar is a form of radar that is used to create images of objects (for instance – landscapes).

In 2003, France launched a national cancer plan. This foresaw the rollout of 60 PET (Positron Emission Tomography)[27] scanners, to detect early stages of cancer. The Réunion/Mayotte health region did not qualify for such a scanner, as it fell below the official threshold of one million. Réunion University therefore joined forces with the *Centre Hospitalier Régional* to create the Cyclotron Réunion Indian Ocean (CYROI). This European Economic Interest Grouping (EEIG),[28] with EU co-funding, purchased a cyclotron for use in medical imaging as well as high-tech research. This project was funded by the ERDF, in a total sum of €20,000,000 and it was operating in the years 2005–2008. The CYROI is a technology platform comprising buildings and equipment, available to businesses or public laboratories in La Réunion and the Indian Ocean, as well as those in Europe and the rest of the world. Its centerpiece is a cyclotron, a compact machine that produces accelerated ion beams for use in nuclear medicine and research.

Opened in 2008 in St-Denis, the CYROI hosted four types of activity: radiopharmaceutical production, medical fundamental research, biotechnology economic development of start-ups, and training and scientific cooperation. The cyclotron produces 18-FDG,[29] a radiotracer that is injected into patients to detect malignant tumors. As a result, as many as 1,500 people from La Réunion or Mayotte can be diagnosed for cancer locally, rather than being evacuated to mainland France for

---

[27] Positron emission tomography is a nuclear medicine functional imaging technique that is used to observe metabolic processes in the body.

[28] A European Economic Interest Grouping is a type of legal entity designed to make it easier for companies in different countries to do business together or to form consortia to take part in EU programs.

[29] Fludeoxyglucose (18F) is a radiopharmaceutical used in the medical imaging modality positron emission tomography.

healthcare. The platform was also harnessed for a wide variety of biomedical research, including metabolic, infectious and emerging diseases, and the promotion of land and marine biodiversity – diversity for which this region is famous worldwide. The Centre for Research and Scientific Monitoring of Infectious Diseases in the Indian Ocean (CRVOI) is also linked to it.

The heavily serviced building is designed to comply with the highest standards demanded by biological, pharmaceutical, animal welfare and nuclear regulatory authorities, including full radiation monitoring system. The building is laid out as two blocks linked by a tropical atrium which is usually open to and which provides an informal break-out space, facilitating encounters between diverse scientific users from which innovation is often born. Technical rooms including the cyclotron are accommodated at the lowest level, while laboratories and offices are in the first floor.

Route des Tamarins

This project sought to upgrade the section of La Réunion's road network, bringing improvements to the lives of residents while respecting the unique infrastructure of the region. Due to the island's beautiful and fragile environment, the project required a great degree of care. Priority was given to environmental considerations when working in this complex landscape. The road in question, Route des Tamarins, was originally constructed in 1987 and is a 2x2 lane route connecting the south and the east via the capital Saint Denis. The road is part of the long-term development program (known as PALT) for the island's national road network. Preserving the environment was a priority in implementing this project. The goal of was to enable the transport infrastructure to be integrated into the region taking account of its ecology, heritage, resources, pollution and security. Given the ecological diversity of the island, many environmental factors need to be taken into account such as protecting the areas around the ravines and the sensitive lagoon areas.

The main aims of the project were to ensure comfort and safety for people travelling the route, to reduce travel times and to protect the environment. Travel between the main population centers of Saint-Pierre, Saint-Benoit and Saint-Denis were greatly improved and traffic blockages reduced. The total investment for this project was €1,091,000,000 with the EU's Regional Development Fund contributing €114,378,201 for the 2007 to 2013 programing period. The project was funded through the priority "Competitiveness of the territory: Organizing the island's territory on the basis of new performance parameters" of the Operational Program "Réunion".

Grand Prado STEP

Among other projects funded by the EU in La Réunion, it was also the location of a five-year project (which lasted from 2007–2013) to update sewage system of its capital city, Saint-Denis, for a growing population, which has already exceeded 160,000 inhabitants. Much of the project concentrates on upgrading the city's sewage treatment plant. The old facilities were limited of handling sewage for the equivalent of 130,000 people. The new plant created for a further 30,000, with expansion potential to 235,000 by 2030. The disinfected discharge from this plant is guaranteed to be equal to "bathing water" quality or better.

Beneficiaries of the project include all local inhabitants, some of which were previously unconnected to a wastewater system.

Total investment for the project "Grand Prado STEP" is €105,935,484, with the EU's ERDF contributing €25,963,550 for the 2007 to 2013 programming period. It comes under the financing priority "Organizing the island's territory on the basis of new performance parameters" of the Operational Program "Réunion".

Energy autonomy of La Réunion

From 1970 to 2012, the population of La Réunion has nearly doubled from 450,000 to almost 840,000 inhabitants. According to EU projections, the population is expected to reach over a million by 2040. In a context of population and economic growth, between 2000 and 2012 primary energy consumption has increased by 3.1% per year and final energy consumption by 2.5% per year. In 2012, 65% of La Réunion's power was generated by fossil fuel (coal and oil) power plants. However, owing to its rich natural environment, this unique EU territory in the Indian Ocean has exceptional potential for renewable power generation. La Réunion is blessed with many types of renewable energy sources (RES) such as solar, wind, geothermal, sea energy (Ocean thermal energy conversion and wave energy), biomass and hydropower. If the island can reach an energetic autonomy by 2030 it would mean a 100% renewable electricity mix by this date. To combat the environmental hazards of continued reliance on fossil fuels, La Réunion has committed to grow sustainably: achieving energy autonomy by 2030 and integrate zero carbon practices into multiples sectors. A top priority is to reach a 100% renewable mix for power. In this context of challenges towards a transition to renewable energy, La Réunion is a source of opportunities in terms of energy development, which can also influence the development of its nearby countries.

La Réunion, the EU, and the Indian Ocean Commission

The Indian Ocean Commission (IOC) is an intergovernmental organization created in 1982 in Port-Louis, Mauritius and institutionalized in 1984 by the *Victoria Agreement* in the Seychelles. The Secretariat of the Commission is located in Mauritius and headed by a Secretary General. The organization also has a system of rotating presidency of each Member State. The IOC's principal mission is to strengthen the ties of friendship between the countries and be a platform of solidarity for the entire population of the Indian-oceanic region. Its mission also includes development, through projects related to sustainability for the region, aimed at protecting the region, improving living conditions of the populations and preserving the very natural resources that the countries depend on. Being an organization regrouping only island states, the IOC has usually championed the cause of small island states in regional and international fora. The IOC works on four pillars which have been adopted in 2005 by the Summit of Heads of States:

1. Political and diplomatic cooperation.

2. Economic and commercial cooperation.

3. Sustainable development in a globalization context.

4. Strengthening of the regional cultural identity.

In the official website of the Commission, which is accessible only in French, there are only two specific missions, which are slightly different from the description in the EU site, yet more detailed. The missions, as described in the IOC site are: a) to put forward the construction and development of all the members of the IOC and to promote their materialistic and financial status, by creating an effective platform to support these states; and b) to provide a framework for its member states to conduct external collective actions of integration and cooperation with the African continent and the rest of the world, as well as sharing multilateral institutions and various donors.

Through the membership of La Réunion (and thus: France), EU partnership with the IOC has been effective for as long as twenty-five years. The successive EDFs have financed programs implemented by the IOC to the tune of €100,000,000, mainly in the area of environment and natural resources. The EU, which is the main development partner of the IOC, has scaled up its assistance to IOC during the last few years, and accounts for more than 80% of total financial support to IOC in 2013. It has some cooperative projects with the IOC concerning the environment and energy. This partnership is also highlighted in the IOC brochure about its relation with the EU, and it also mentions the EU important role in the development of the IOC member states, all of which are islands.

Biodiversity

The €15,000,000 program for the Coastal, Marine and Island Specific Biodiversity Management, signed in January 2013, aims at developing and strengthening over five years the national and regional capacities for sustainable participatory management of coastal, marine and island specific biodiversity in the islands states and coastal states of the East Africa and Indian Ocean regions, namely: Comoros, Madagascar, Mauritius, Seychelles, Kenya and Tanzania. La Réunion participates in the program on its own funds (notably from the ERDF). Five main results are expected from the program:

1. Improved and harmonized policies and legal and institutional frameworks across the region for the sustainable use of biodiversity.

2. Enhanced education sensitization, communication and information tools for the management of the use of biodiversity, in support of decision makers at regional, national and community levels.

3. Improved systems for networking and exchange of data, statistics, and other biodiversity related information.

4. Biodiversity Thematic Centers created or enhanced for the exchange of information, experiences and best practices in the sustainable use of the biodiversity.

5. Enhanced contribution of biodiversity to sustainable economic development and sustainable livelihoods across the region.

Energy

The €15,000,000 program for the RE (Renewable Energy) development and EE (Energy Efficiency) improvements in IOC Member states, signed in June 2013, aims at establishing the conditions for the development, investment and sustainable management of renewable energy and improvements in the efficiency of energy use in the IOC region. La Réunion participates in the program on its own funds (notably from the ERDF). The main results which expected from the program are:

1. A regional IOC strategy focused on human resources development and institutional building is agreed and implementation started.

2. The regulatory and business environments for RE based grid-connected electricity generation are improved, and wind/solar resource data bases further developed.

3. Government agencies and private investors capabilities are developed to design, engineer, construct and operate decentralized electric power/energy systems based on RE.

4. Energy efficiency standards and labels are developed and implemented in most IOC member countries for all categories of buildings and for household appliances and equipment with major impact on electricity consumption and peak load.

La Réunion as a Forward Presence Bases of the EU

The importance of La Réunion to the EU is not only in the diplomatic aspects, but also in the military one. Thus, the island can be used to demonstrate the implementation of the CFSP as a "soft power" instrument and as a "hard power" instrument. Although in the next chapter, the British Falkland Islands will be used to explain the security policy of the EU in the overseas in more detail, here is the chance to give another example of the importance of the OMRs to the EU, in the aspects of diplomacy and security. La Réunion is used by the French navy (French: *Marine nationale*) as a Forward Presence Bases, which is the name of the EU member states overseas military logistical supply bases. European Forward Presence Bases function similarly to their US counterparts, the Forward Operating Sites. But in the case of France and the UK, these bases can either be sovereign or foreign-hosted. The former are normally permanent, and have two functions:

Firstly, as a centre of operations for protecting and upholding sovereignty over the overseas territory in which the Foreign Presence Base is located; and secondly, projecting power into the surrounding geographic region. Sovereign Foreign Presence Bases include La Réunion, Diego Garcia, New Caledonia or the Falkland Islands. In comparison with these, or the Military Stations, the foreign-hosted Forward Presence Bases are often less permanent and more transitory. They can be moved and relocated as events and conditions dictate, a good example being France's geostrategic push into the Persian Gulf with the opening of a new Foreign Presence Base in the United Arab Emirates (UAE) in 2009. As the world's economy relies on sea routes for 90% of trade, piracy in the Indian Ocean and the Gulf of Aden has made this issue more pressing in recent years, and affected delivery of humanitarian aid to Somalia. Thus, EU military presence in Réunion helps naval forces to equip themselves with supplies, and carry on to their operations.

The French Army (French: *Armée de terre*) counts 750 personnel, namely the 2nd Regiment of Marine Infantry Parachutists in Réunion and a Detachment from the Foreign Legion in Mayotte. The Navy comprises 430 people, a naval station in Reunion Island with two "P400" patrol boats, an "Austral" patrol boat, a maritime affairs patrol, one "Batral" ferry, a Gendarmerie maritime patrol and a fusilier detachment. In Mayotte there is a marine detachment with a servitude high-speed motorboat, a boat for transporting material and a high-speed motorboat for coastal maritime surveillance (Gendarmerie). The French Air Force (French: *Armée de l'air*) includes 280 personnel in Réunion, including two "Transall" and two "Fennec".

France's contingent in the Indian Ocean (ALINDIEN) includes three joint command facilities; one based in Réunion, another in Djibouti and a third one is permanently based aboard a command ship. ALINDIEN contributes to the peacekeeping and stabilization of the Indian Ocean, contributing to coalition enterprises outside the Persian Gulf (i.e. Operation Active Endeavour),[30] as well as maritime security, humanitarian operations and defence diplomacy. ALINDIEN's means include a command and resupply boat with its own headquarters (with thirty-five personnel), two surveillance frigates based in Réunion, a marine commando unit and a maritime surveillance plane based in Djibouti.

Chapter Summary

For five decades (from 1957 to 2007) the OMRs were considered as unimportant to the EU, as tools of foreign affairs or as military strategic locations. In the past ten years, however, this perspective has changed, and nowadays the OMRs are considered as highly valuable to promote the EU's CFSP in South America, the Caribbean region and the Indian Ocean region. Despite its view of the OMRs for a long time, the EU had conducted some cooperative projects with non-EU countries, based on the locations of its OMRs, in the case study examined in this chapter – La Réunion. The EU invested, and still is investing a

---

[30] Operation Active Endeavour is a maritime operation launched by NATO on October 4, 2001. It operates in the Mediterranean Sea and is designed to prevent the movement of terrorists or weapons of mass destruction

significant amount of money in the development of its OMRs and increasing its influence on nearby countries, by making its investment profitable to them as well.

However, one might ask why, then, there is no English, German, Spanish or any other language translation to the IOC website, which is working in close cooperation with the EU, and an OMR of the EU is one of its members. An attempt to answer this question will be given in the fourth chapter of this thesis, which deals with the integration within the EU, and how it can be reflected in the CFSP. Another reason for the investment of the EU in its OMRs in the recent years is their lack of ability to grow ecumenically by themselves. The economic growth in Réunion can be weakened by its dependency on the final consumption of the household and by the weight of the construction sector. Generally speaking, it also lacks competitiveness compared with the countries of the Indian Ocean. Infrastructures are also a weak point, the island is extremely remote from other countries and EU and the cost of transportation is particularly high. Demographic data also shows the pledge of the population growth and density on the sustainable development perspectives and on the social welfare (unemployment, illiteracy, ageing population).

Unemployment is a major problem in Réunion, and it reached a total of 30% in 2014, when among young people it reached almost 60%. According to *Le Monde*, one of France's most popular daily newspapers, 42% of the population in Réunion lived below the poverty line in 2010. The EU is attempting in its *Europe 2020* agenda to implement an inclusive growth, which means empowering people through high levels of employment, investing in skills, fighting poverty and modernizing labor markets, training and social protection systems so as to help people anticipate and manage change, and build a cohesive society. It is also essential that the benefits of economic growth spread to all parts of the Union, including its outermost regions, thus strengthening territorial cohesion. It is about ensuring access and opportunities for all throughout the lifecycle. Europe needs to make full use of its labor potential to face the challenges of an ageing population and rising global competition. Policies to promote gender equality will be needed to increase labor force participation thus adding to growth and social cohesion.

There is a global awareness of the need for radical changes in the direction of a more competitive and market-oriented economy and that the oversized public sector cannot continue to grow as a response to the crisis. The strategic vision is that regional development needs to be based on a balanced integration of different sectors in which each contributes to the regional income, rather than following a specialized pattern with one sector acting as leading factor for development. The strategy aims at sustainable development both by lowering dependence on fossil fuels for energy use and by changing the consumption and investment patterns by developing more knowledge intensive manufacturing and services, and being a laboratory for renewable energies experimenting and testing processes and plants.

There is also a strong and explicit consensus among local actors on strategic objectives. The latest expression of this consensus is to be found in "La Réunion Île Verte" (French for: the green island Réunion) and in the Regional Innovation Strategy.[31] Some of these projects are

---

[31] The Regional Innovation Strategy is a strategic policy of the OECD to improve the

quite precise and are accompanied by preliminary studies. All proposals need to be carefully confronted with the economic analysis in order to assess their adequacy with the determinants of growth and to be discussed with public authorities to build up a concrete, detailed and realistic strategy. In the end, the OMRs are a good infrastructure for the EU to spread its ideas world-wide, and gain political influence in regions which were so far beyond its reach. If the EU would be capable of speaking in one voice, according to its CFSP, it might even strengthen the integration between the EU members states themselves, as all parties will have something to gain from it.

---

economic status of poor regions within the OECD member states.

CHAPTER THREE

The EU's Security Policy

The previous chapter dealt with the foreign policy of the EU, as part of its CFSP, and the use of "soft power" tools by the EU in order to achieve better political influence in various regions in the world, through projects and investments in its OMRs. This chapter aims to present the second approach of the EU as part of its CFSP – the security policy or the "hard power" tools, i.e. its [naval] military strength, by the use of it OCTs.

The idea of uniting the military interests of the EU member states was initiated by the former French Prime Minister, René Pleven, in 1950, before the EEC even came to existence. However it was the Franco-British Summit in St. Malo, France, in December 1998, which marked the starting point of a real cooperation in the area of security and defence at the EU level (until then, this kind of cooperation was handled by NATO). In this summit, the governments of the two most important military powers in Europe urged the EU to set up "the capacity for autonomous action, backed by credible forces, the means to decide to use them and a readiness to do so". This call resulted mainly from the bitter experience of the Balkan wars in the 1990s,[32] which demonstrated that although the EU had more than two million soldiers available, it was not able to generate a force from this pool.

It is interesting to notice that the St. Malo Summit was held solely by two countries (France and the UK), when non other EU member state

---

[32] These wars are: the war in Slovenia (1991), the Croatian War of Independence (1991–1995) and the Bosnian War (1992–1995).

was invited, and that it took place one year after the *Treaty of Amsterdam* as signed, the treaty which introduced for the first time the OMRs and OCTs. France and the UK are also the two countries who hold the most overseas regions and territories among the EU member states (70% in total for both countries). Though this summit dealt not only with the overseas security issues, as part of this thesis, this chapter will present the security policy of the EU implemented specifically in its overseas territories through a case study of one OCT – the British Falkland Islands, and examine if it complies with the EU's CFSP and the EU's Common Security and Defence Policy (CSDP).[33]

Choosing the Falkland Islands out of all other possible options, of which eleven are British, was due to the following reasons:

1. The Falkland Islands are a home of a very large military installation of the British army. They possess two hardened runways, 2,590 and 1,525 meters long, which are capable of taking trans-Atlantic aircraft, including civilian aeroplanes. There is also a deep-water naval station, called Mare Harbor, within the facility, which is frequented by vessels from the Royal Navy that are used to patrol the South Atlantic.

2. As mentioned above, Britain is one of the two strongest armies of the EU member states (alongside France), and the Falkland Islands are a Forward Presence Bases of the UK. Thus, just like La Réunion, it is a centre of operations for the Royal Navy, and it is also a supply center for both the Royal Navy and the Royal Air Force (the RAF).

---

[33] The CSDP is a major element of the EU's CFSP and is the domain of EU policy covering defence and military aspects, as well as civilian crisis management.

3. The Falklands War of 1982 put these islands in the spot light, challenging in the same time the European security policy, foreign policy and internal integration. This war will set as an example for European unity (or disunity) at a time of military crisis overseas.

European Colonialism in the Falkland Islands

The Falkland Islands are located at around 52°S in the southwestern Atlantic, c. 450 km north-east of Tierra del Fuego, and 600 km east of southern Patagonian Argentina. There are hundreds of small islands, and two larger ones, known as East and West Falkland that are separated by Falkland Sound, a sea passage (or a sea strait) c. 15 km wide that runs in a northeast-southwest direction. The total land area of the islands is around 12,000 km^2. The Falkland Islands had no indigenous population prior to their settlement by the European settlers in the mid-eighteenth century. The British first came to the Falkland Islands in 1765, and withdrew them in 1774, after the break out of the American Revolution. By that time the British, the French and the Spaniards periodically had garrisons in the Islands until 1811, when all the garrisons were withdrawn.

In 1832, an Argentine military garrison landed in an attempt to establish Argentine sovereignty over the Falkland Islands (which they called *Islas Malvinas*, as the Spaniards did), disregarding the British claim of 67 years prior. Less than three months later the Royal Navy evicted the Argentine military garrison with no loss of life. In 1834 a small permanent British administration was established. With an increasing population, in 1845 Stanley was founded, and remains the islands' Capital to this day. During the time of the British Empire, the

Falkland Islands were considered as a "fortress colony", whose imperial function had been to watch over vital sea lanes and provide links in a chain of world-wide communications. In the era of decolonization, however, they posed special problem, as their function was no longer needed as much as before. Their British control today is one of the "leftovers" of that British Empire, after its last major round of decolonization in the 1960s.

The EU and Britain's Overseas Territories

All of the British overseas territories, except Gibraltar (which is an overseas territory in British perspective, but it is located in mainland Europe), are not part of the EU. This fact is not to be taken lightly, since even the British Sovereign Base Areas (SBA) in the Republic of Cyprus[34] (a member state of the EU), are not part of the union. Furthermore, in both the UK's and Cyprus' agreements of accessions to the EU it was stated clearly that the SBA – Akrotiri and Dhekelia – will not become EU territories, and will remain solely under the control of the British government. Theoretically, all parts of the EU member states within the EU are to be subjected to EU law unless a special clause excluded them from it. Such is the case of the SBA. To emphasize the inclusion of territories within the EU – even The Turkish Republic of Northern Cyprus, though not recognized as a member state, and is considered "an occupied EU territory", and "a part of the EU where the Union's law cannot be enforced", thus its membership in the Union is suspended.

---

[34] The Sovereign Base Areas of Akrotiri and Dhekelia, is a British Overseas Territory on the island of Cyprus. The areas, which include British military bases and installations, as well as other land, were retained by the British under the 1960 treaty of independence for the Republic of Cyprus.

Therefore it is outside the common internal market yet the EU has special legal arrangements for North Cyprus which makes it a territory within the EU. The SBA, however, has a special clause to keep it *out* of the EU.

The official reason for the British request to exclude these parts of Cyprus from the EEC, and from its future enlargement under the EU, was due to their "non-economic" character, but this fact, however, does not apply to many other British overseas territories (for instance Anguilla, Bermuda, or the Cayman Islands). It simply seems Britain wishes not to have the EU intervening its overseas policy, and when examining the Falklands War, it will be shown British government, under the leadership of Prime Minister Margaret Thatcher, preferred the EU's diplomatic support in the UN rather than any military aid. Furthermore, the UK did not ask for the aid of NATO, by activating Article 5 of the NATO agreement, though the Argentine aggression against the Falkland Islands could be seen as an invasion to a NATO member state's territory. Another exception of the British overseas territories (including Gibraltar) in the EU context is their exemption from using the Euro as their currency. This is in contrast to the French OMRs, which have the Euro as their official currency. This exemption is due to a clause the UK (and Denmark) has in their agreements of accessions, allowing them (and their overseas territories) to opt-out the common currency of the EU.

But the British themselves are not the sole reason the EU has little influence, if any, on the OCTs of the UK. Bermuda, for instance resists any association with the EU, and the government of the Turks and Caicos Islands feels the same way. The British Virgin Islands and the

Cayman Islands (two OCTs whose main income is from being tax shelters) struggle the EU to prevent its financial regulations from applying on them. In the case of the Caribbean overseas territories of the UK, the attitude is relatively different from the Dutch or French territories, who seek more integration with EU institutions. As for the EU itself, it wishes to include all OMRs and OCTs, including Britain's in its CFSP as it sees these territories as "strategically important outposts, spread all over the world as proponents of the EU's values". The Falkland Islands will be used as an example which shows if the EU is able to execute these ambitions as part of its security policy.

The EU's Security Policy and CSDP

The EU member states have committed themselves to a common foreign and security policy for the EU. The European Security and Defence Policy (ESDP) or Common Security and Defence Policy (CSDP) aims to strengthen the EU's external ability to act by developing civilian and military capabilities in conflict prevention and crisis management. To influence policies violating international law or human rights, or policies disrespectful of the rule of law or democratic principles, the EU has designed sanctions of a diplomatic or economic nature. The point of the CFSP and CSDP is that the EU would be more coherent in its security policy, by acting as one body with common goals. The challenge the EU faces are how to bring together the different instruments and capabilities it has, which can have an impact on the EU's security and on that of third countries. Security, as the EU sees it, is the first condition for development.

The TFEU, which came into force in December 2009, was a cornerstone in the development of the CSDP. The treaty includes both a mutual assistance and a solidarity clause and allowed for the creation of the European External Action Service (EEAS) under the authority of the High Representative of the Union for Foreign Affairs & Security Policy/Vice-President of the European Commission (HR/VP). The two distinct functions of the newly created post give the HR/VP the possibility to bring all the necessary EU assets together and to apply a "comprehensive approach" to EU crisis management. In many ways the development of CSDP over the last decade has been defined by its relationship with NATO. It is stating the obvious to say that the EU-NATO relationship matters because of the strategic importance of the transatlantic relationship, not least because NATO remains the guarantor of European security for its member states. This has made the EU's relationship with NATO a much more strategic and political challenge than the EU's interaction with other international organizations, such as the UN.

Map of the Overseas Military Installations of the EU Member States

Since 1999, some observers have wondered if the development of CSDP might mean that NATO would eventually become irrelevant, if American and European strategic interests diverged. So far, this has not been the case. NATO is still relevant, while CSDP has developed in its own direction. The CSDP defines itself as a broad and comprehensive international security policy, with access to both civil and military instruments. In other words, the CSDP is potentially meant to do everything but collective defence – the *raison d'être* of NATO.

The importance of a maritime strategy

The CSDP is a general guideline of action of the EU during a time of crisis. For this thesis, however, it is important to focus more on the EU's Maritime Security Strategy. But before it could be fully explained, an explanation should be given of what is, at all, a maritime strategy. A distinction is therefore to be made between a naval strategy and a maritime strategy. While the naval strategy can be defined by as the science of using naval forces (ships, submarines etc.) in battle, the maritime strategy is the science of using both naval and non-naval sources of power at sea. The British navalist Sir Julian S. Corbett[35] defined the maritime strategy as "the principles that govern a war in which the sea is a substantial factor". In his book *Some Principles of Maritime Strategy*, Corbett also adds that: "naval strategy is but that part of it which determines the movements of the fleet when maritime strategy has determined what part the fleet must play in relation to the action of the land forces; for it scarcely needs saying that it is almost

---

[35] Sir Julian Stafford Corbett (1854–1922) was a British naval historian and geostrategist, whose works helped shape the British Royal Navy's reforms during the late 19th century and early 20th century.

impossible that a war can be decided by naval action alone." This strategy can be exampled by the American Revolutionary War: the British had commanded the sea, a factor which gave them a great advantage over the Americans. Thus, they enjoyed mobility of troops which was denied from the Americans, who used primitive land communications. This fact allowed the British to capture strategic ports including the city of New York. It was only the arrival of the French which eventually saved the Americans.

Being able to control the sea is an important factor of making a nation (or the EU) a maritime empire. Throughout the centuries, even small countries like the Netherlands and Portugal or the Italian city-states, have gained great political power as a result of their naval power and control of strategic islands. The greatest and most powerful empire of all times, mostly due to its control of the sea and ocean – was the British Empire.

The EU's Maritime Security Strategy

The European Union Maritime Security Strategy (EUMSS) covers both the internal and external aspects of the Union's maritime security. It serves as comprehensive framework, contributing to a stable and secure global maritime domain, in accordance with the European Security Strategy (ESS), while ensuring coherence with EU policies, in particular the Integrated Maritime Policy (IMP), and the Internal Security Strategy (ISS). The EUMSS has been adopted through a comprehensive and coordinated process whose major milestones are the Council Conclusions of April 26, 2010, the Council Conclusions on integration of Maritime Surveillance of May 23, 2011, the Limassol

Declaration of October 7, 2012, the European Council Conclusions of December 2013 and the Joint Communication by the European Commission and the High Representative of March 6, 2014. As for the IMP, it sets out a coherent strategy to enhance the sustainable development of maritime sectors. Coordination is necessary to manage the increasing impact of maritime activities on each other and on the environment, to ensure the safety and security of European citizens and to maintain a qualified workforce.

European maritime policy also faces changing conditions. One of the main challenges is the anthropogenic release of carbon dioxide, leading to ocean warming, ocean acidification and rising sea levels. A particular concern for Europe would be a slowing of the Gulf Stream in the Atlantic Ocean. Based on the EU's founding values of human rights, freedom and democracy, the purpose of the EUMSS is to secure the maritime security interests of the EU and its member states against a plethora of risks and threats in the global maritime domain. This is achieved in a cross-sectoral, comprehensive, coherent and cost-efficient way, in conformity with existing treaties, national and EU legislation and international law, in particular the United Nations Convention on the Law of the Sea (UNCLOS) and other relevant conventions and instruments. In the present geopolitical era, the security and prosperity of the EU are increasingly dependent on its ability to project power into the maritime domain. Today, up to 90% of the EU's trade comes leaves by the sea. Any credible strategy to implement the much needed diversification of energy supplies (most notably gas) will also rely on the security of the maritime arena. Furthermore, the EU's ability to reach other areas of the world – particularly militarily – will also remain dependent on its unfettered access to the sea.

As a result of these facts, the EUMSS is based on the following guiding principles:

1. *Cross-sectoral approach*: all partners from civilian and military authorities and actors (law enforcement, border control, customs and fisheries inspection, environmental authorities, maritime administration, research and innovation, navies or other maritime forces, coast guards, intelligence agencies), as well as EU agencies, to industry (shipping, security, communication, capability support) need to cooperate better, respecting each other's internal organization.

2. *Functional integrity*: the EUMSS does not affect the respective competences of the Union and its member states in the areas covered. It is also without prejudice to the competences, sovereign rights and jurisdiction of member states over maritime zones in accordance with relevant international law, including UNCLOS. The mandates, responsibilities and interests of member states need to be fully taken into account, building upon existing policies and instruments and making best use of existing capabilities at national and EU level, while avoiding to create new structures, legislation, additional administrative burden, as well as the requirement for additional funding.

3. *Respect for rules and principles*: respect for international law, human rights and democracy and full compliance with UNCLOS, the applicable bilateral treaties and the values enshrined therein are the cornerstones of the EUMSS and key principles for rules-based good governance at sea. The EU and its member states support the settlement of maritime disputes arising from the interpretation and application of

UNCLOS through competent international courts and tribunals provided therein, which play an important role in implementing the rule of law at sea.

4. *Maritime multilateralism*: while respecting the institutional framework and the decision-making autonomy of the EU, cooperation with all relevant international partners and organizations, in particular the UN and NATO, and coordination with existing international and regional fora in the maritime domain are essential.

The main objective of the EUMSS remains, however, to enhance capacity for conflict prevention and crisis response, prevention of conflicts and incidents, risk mitigation and the protection of the EU's marine environmental status, the security of the Union's external borders, as well as its critical maritime infrastructure. This objective depends on a high degree of preparation, anticipation and responsiveness. A set of interlocking actions is already in place, but the EU and its member states can improve their responsiveness and resilience.

EU's overseas bases types

Before "diving" into the example of the Falklands War as part of the CFSP, an explanation on the type of overseas bases the EU possesses overseas is to be given. The EU constitutes the second largest collection of overseas military facilities in the world (after the US) and its basing presence is dynamic and subject to change with new geopolitical realities. An example which will be more detailed over the next few pages is the UK's considerable upgrade of its garrison in the

Falkland Islands, as a result of the 1982 war. The EU member states bases are divided into four categories, as follows:

Homeland Installations: The "hub" – the Homeland Installations – contains the Permanent Joint Headquarters and the major air stations, naval dockyards and barracks, such as Portsmouth (in the UK) and Toulon (in France), or the air stations of Brize Norton (in the UK) or Istres (in France).

Military Stations: The "spokes" include those military facilities like Ascension Island, Akrotiri (one of the SBA bases) or Djibouti.[36] These operate as "lily pads", or Military Stations, allowing military forces from the Homeland Installations to move further afield. During the Falklands War, for example, the British stations in Gibraltar and Ascension Island allowed the Royal Navy and the Royal Air Force to reach the South Atlantic more rapidly and with less need to send costly relays of refueling ships or tanker aircraft to supply equipment on the front line.

Forward Presence Bases: At the end of the "spokes" are the Forward Presence Bases, which are effectively the termini of the overseas military basing infrastructure and logistical supply capacity. European Forward Presence Bases function similarly to their US counterparts, the Forward Operating Sites. But in the cases of France and the UK, these bases can either be sovereign or foreign-hosted.

Strategic Projection Vessels: The Homeland Installations, the Military Stations, and some of the Forward Presence Bases, all operate to keep afloat another, somewhat unique, category of military bases:

---

[36] This is where the French *13ᵉ demi-brigade de Légion étrangère* headquarters was located before moving to the *Camp de la Paix* in Abu Dhabi.

those that float. The strategic projection vessels include aircraft carriers and amphibious assault vessels, as well as logistical support ships and cruise missile firing submarines, thereby reducing the infrastructural imprint of the static maritime infrastructure. These unique vessels can then be deployed into almost any theatre for many different purposes, ranging from full-scale warfare, to humanitarian assistance operations and search and rescue. They afford their owners with several hundred square meters of floating airfield, which can move around as circumstances dictate, reducing the likelihood of attack.

In all, EU member states maintain and operate sixteen major military installations. France has nine overseas military facilities, five of which are sovereign installations, whereas foreign countries host four. The UK has military installations in twenty-eight different territories and countries overseas. Of these, only six can be described as large military installations, while the others account for a myriad of training, recruit and support facilities. All major British overseas bases are located on sovereign territory. Other EU member states, such as Spain, the Netherlands and Germany, have or had military facilities overscas: Spain has a permanent naval dockyard in thc Canary Islands (an OMR of the EU), whereas Germany and the Netherlands operated a small temporary staging airfield in Tajikistan for the supply of their forces in Afghanistan (from 2001 to 2014) after the September 11 attacks on the US in 2001.

The Falklands War and the EU's Security Policy

Although the Falklands War (or *Guerra de las Malvinas* in Spanish) was fought before the creation of the CFSP, it can give some hints of how the EU handles a security crisis overseas, and also the attitude of Britain/the UK towards the EU in these situations. In short, the EU prefers do use diplomacy over violent force, and would tolerate violent actions of one of its member states only as long as they're defensive and "proportionate" to the situation.

Background

Since the UK's final seizure of the Falkland Islands in 1833, it had governed the islands without interruption from any other state, although the Argentine government argues it has maintained a claim over the islands since 1832. Indeed, in 1965 Argentina even took the Falklands case to the UN, which sporadically sponsored negotiations between the two claimants. However these negotiations made little progress, as neither side was willing to concede on the central issue of eventual sovereignty (each country for its own reasons). Nevertheless, for 150 years, the dispute remained a diplomatic issue to be dealt with in a civilized way. Therefore, the Argentine invasion to the islands caught the British Prime Minister, Margaret Thatcher, and the British People themselves by surprise. However, Thatcher's decision to retaliate and go to war with Argentina was largely support by the British popular mood. This might have been a result of British inner-feeling of losing their once-great-empire and seeing the world's political hegemony move to Washington and Moscow.

Thatcher, who was the leader of the British Conservative Party since 1975 and the prime minister of Britain from 1979 (and until 1991), and who was nicknamed the "Iron Lady", was not about to give up the last remains of the British Empire without a "proper" fight. The war broke out in a time the British Empire seemed to be at its last gleam of twilights, but under the given circumstances and with pressure from home to boost national moral and pride, the British would not have given up even these remote islands, a symbol of its glorious past – even in the cost of going to war with Argentina. It should be pointed out that the Falklands War was the first militant act of Britain in defending what was left of its empire, since the failing operation in Suez in 1956. A military victory (which the UK eventually gained) was important more for the British internal affairs, than for its international ones. In a way, the war was Britain's last attempt to pretend (mainly for itself) and act as an independent "empire". However the Falklands War confirmed nothing more than the primordial survival of an imperial nerve within British society than of the existing of the British mighty force in international affairs.

The EEC reaction to the war

On the morning of Friday, April 2, 1982, Argentine forces mounted amphibious landings off the Falkland Islands, following their occupation of South Georgia and the South Sandwich Islands two weeks earlier, on March 19, before the Falklands War began. The British Permanent Representative to the UN, Sir Anthony Parsons, immediately called an emergency session of the Security Council. He demanded a vote within 24 hours on a resolution drawn up by the UK, demanding an immediate ceasefire and a full withdrawal of all military forces from the islands captured by Argentina. In addition to its diplomatic efforts with the UN, the UK formally asked the EEC member states, through the European Commission (EC) to impose economic sanctions on Argentina. British officials described intensive discussions with EEC member states as the centerpiece of diplomatic efforts to isolate Argentina. British diplomatic efforts focused on the Federal Republic of Germany (West Germany), Argentina's largest trade partner in the Community and a significant source of military goods to the Argentine army. The British efforts were successful, as Austria, Belgium, France, West Germany, the Netherlands, and Switzerland (who was not EEC member state) responded immediately by embargoing arms sales to Argentina.

The war had made the European Political Cooperation (EPC), the forum in which the member states sought to coordinate their foreign policies, more power than it had before. The actions of the EPC during the crisis, the first real crisis it had to endure since its establishment in 1970, marked a step of importance in the gradual evolution of European foreign policy and internal integration. The European solidarity, however, did not last long. Until April 25 the Falklands dispute remained mainly a matter of diplomacy rather than military confrontation, but on that date, British task force sent from Gibraltar, reached South Georgia and recaptured it. Britain would have had sufficient forces in the area by April 30 when it had started to enforce a 200-mile (c. 320 km) blockade.[37]

The following day, May 1, fighting began in the Falklands with British air bombers attacking airfields on the islands. On the night of May 2 and 3, a British submarine sank the Argentine Cruiser *General Belgrano*, which was outside the declared exclusion zone. More than 300 Argentine sailors were killed in this attack. This action shocked

---

[37] A blockade is an effort executed in wartime to cut off supplies, war material or communications from a particular area. A blockade should not be confused with an embargo or sanctions, which are legal barriers to trade.

most of the world, as it realized the potential for widespread casualties in the Falklands. The sinking had a negative impact on sympathy for the British in Europe, where many felt that Britain had acted too aggressively and with a disproportionate force. As a result, Ireland called for an end to EEC sanctions against Argentina. The sinking of the *General Belgrano* might be considered as a military victory to the UK, but it suffered a political defeat within the public opinion of the EEC member states, which had supported it until then. As far as the other EEC member states saw the situation in the Falklands, any military action which was not self-evidently of defensive purposes, became an outrage. The member states of the EEC had hoped that economic pressure would be sufficient to prevent Argentina from going to war with Britain, but they also believed that the shared values they had with the UK would prevent it to act aggressively.

Map of British task forces' movement during the Falklands War

The Falklands War was the first real test of the fragile unity of the member states of the EEC and to the reaction of its policy makers in a time of [military] crisis. The preferable course, as it was shown above, was to handle the crisis first with the "soft power" tools, before making the use of violent force. Evidently, the UK had received the support of the EEC prior to its decision to react militarily, and even at the first actions of war. However the sinking of the *General Belgrano* caused the British to lose much of their support within the EEC. Though the public opinion in Europe could tolerate a certain level of [defensive] force initiated by the UK, this incident was considered as an excessive use of force, and therefore intolerable by the European public opinion.

The conclusion of the events in the Falklands is that the EU security policy in the overseas is to repeal invaders from EU member states' territories, but with the use of as minimal force as possible, in order to prevent a high death-toll from both sides. It is reasonable to assume that given a certain political atmosphere, the EU decision makers would decide not to use any force, in case of an invasion to one of its OCTs at least, as these islands are not really part of the Union. It is hard to predict, however, how the EU decision makers might act in the case of an act of war in one of its OMRs, which have the same legal status as every region within continental Europe. A possible example can be given, though, by examining the "miniature war" between Spain and Morocco in 2002.

The clash erupted over an island called "Isla de Perejil" by the Spanish and "Leila Island" by the Moroccans. This island is part of a series of Spanish possessions in Morocco, among them are the two autonomous cities of Spain, Ceuta and Melilla (which are part of the EU),[38] that date back to the fifteenth century. In 1960, Spain and morocco signed an agreement that neither country would establish a permanent presence on Perejil. Accordingly, Spain withdrew the island's last permanent inhabitants, Spain's Foreign Legionnaires,[39] in 1998. However, on July 11, 2002, Morocco stormed the island and ended the forty years-old *status quo*. Spain quickly reacted with an invasion and returned the situation to the *status quo ante*, thus avoiding a Moroccan *fait accompli*[40] on the island. The incident on Isla de Perejil did not escalate, but would the EU public opinion tolerate the use of violent force on an uninhabited island, had the Spaniards were to mimic the British action in 1982? It is hard to tell, but it is very likely for the answer to be: "no".

The CFSP and in the OCTs

Despite the conflict between the UK and Argentina in the Falkland Islands in 1982, the strategic value of the OCTs as the Union's overseas outposts and the potential risks they pose to the EU (such as a military escalation), are not reflected in the ESS of 2003 and its review of 2008. They are also not mentioned in the EUMSS in any way. This neglect is even more surprising considering that a key characteristic of most OCTs is that in addition to being islands, they are also peripheral regions situated on the EU's external borders, and thus they are more exposed to

---

[38] Ceuta and Melilla are part of the EU, yet they are not considered as OMRs, but as "Special Cases".

[39] Spain's Foreign Legionnaires is a unit of the Spanish Army which was raised in the 1920s to serve as part of Spain's Army of Africa. The unit is the Spanish equivalent of the French Foreign Legion.

[40] From French: accomplished fact; something that has already happened and is thus unlikely to be reversed, a done deal.

specific risks: proximity to conflict zones, exposure to clandestine immigration, vulnerability to accidental or deliberate marine pollution, etc. In some cases, their remoteness, insularity, small size, difficult topography and climate, demographic fragmentation and economic dependence on a few products weigh heavy on OCTs' structural social and economic conditions and restrain their development severely.

However, British defence policy after the war illustrates the strategic rationale of the state's own behavior, but can also give a glance on the EU's security policy in the overseas. As a result of the armed conflict in the Falkland Islands the UK decided to upgrade its garrison in the South Atlantic considerably. The idea behind the British government's decision to increase the garrison on the islands was that the war was a test not only for the British government, but also for European integration and NATO. A less decisive retaliation might have exposed a weakness in the security policy of the UK and the EEC/EU.

A reporter of *The Wall Street Journal* described Thatcher's decision to go to war as a reasonable call: "Mrs. Thatcher fought for pride and for principle, which are not such small things in life or affairs of state. She fought because the alternative was to demonstrate that British sovereignty was an easily violable thing, and that the loyalty 1,800 British subjects had sworn to the crown would not be reciprocated." Even before the conflict has ended, Prime Minister Thatcher had commissioned Lord Shackleton,[41] to produce a further study in the light of the new situation. Shackleton presented in effect a blue-print for the economic future of the islands and most of his

---

[41] Edward Arthur Alexander Shackleton, Baron Shackleton (1911–1994), was a British geographer and politician

recommendations were implemented in the succeeding years. It was also required to design a structure for the defence of the Islands which was reasonably economical yet offered a deterrent to possible attack.

The solution chosen was a strategic airport built at Mount Pleasant, about 35 miles from Stanley, where a garrison could be stationed. The first runway was opened in May 1985 and a regular air service, operated by the British RAF, became feasible, open to military and a few civilian passengers. This made it possible to minimize the number of troops in the islands and rely on rapid reinforcement of the garrison in times of tension. Though the EU itself did not invest in the military development of the Falkland Islands, it did, however, helped in upgrading the French overseas collectivities (French: *collectivité d'outre-mer* or COM)[42] in the Pacific Ocean – French Polynesia and Wallis and Futuna – due to their military and economic value to the EU. In general, the EU's policy when it comes to the OCTs is to leave the management of territorial development to the countries governing them.

Chapter Summary

It emerges that security policy of the EU is more difficult to implement than its foreign policy, for several reasons. The main reason is the EU member states', and especially the UK, wish to handle their security issues on their own. This view also has the support of the public opinion within the EU. Eurobarometer surveys since 1989 have shown the support of more than 60% of EU citizens in a common foreign policy for the union. In some years, this support was as high as 70%.

---

[42] The overseas collectivities of France are a lower administrative divisions comparing to the DOM.

However, the defence policy did not receive quite the same amount of support. As a matter of fact, respondents appear to be almost split between supporting an EU-made and a national defence policy, when in most years the national Government wins.

The security policy in the OCTs, as it was shown through the case study of the Falkland Islands, is a problematic issue, due to their legal status within the EU. Taking into consideration some of them are used as military outposts of their governing states, and adding to it the general public opinion on who should handle the security policy within the EU, and it is understandable why the EU institutions find it very hard to implement its security policy overseas. The CFSP was meant to use as a tool of increasing integration within its members in the mattes of foreign affairs, just as the European Monetary Union (EMU) has done so economically. The results, however, are the same, while in the economic unity it was France and Germany who played a decisive role, in the CFSP it was France and the UK.

The wars in the Balkans in the early 1990s might have the same effect upon the EU's security future as German unification has had upon its monetary one. In both cases the final goal is the same: to increase integration between the member states, by creating a mechanism which would help them speak with one coherent voice. Some scholars believe that if the CFSP launched at Maastricht was to be taken seriously, it requires a significant, autonomous military force and institutional capacity.

CHAPTER FOUR

The Overseas Territories and European Integration

The TEU envisaged three pillars for EU. The first was the European Community itself – that is to say, the obligations, rights, and common activities contained in the EEC Treaties. The second and third pillars fell outside the scope of the EEC Treaties altogether: interstate cooperation through the CFSP and the Justice and Home Affairs (JHA).[43] Through the implementation of the CFSP, including the eventual forming of a common defence policy, the EU hoped to achieve an international identity. The European Council was to define "common positions" and the member states were to ensure that their individual foreign policies conformed to them. The European Council then established guidelines on which the Council of Ministers could decide on joint action. These joint actions were meant to help the EU "speak" in one voice, thus increasing the integration among its member states, an integration which would made the EU a stronger union, and it foreign policy and security policy more coherent to the world.

So far, chapters 2 and 3 presented the way the EU is implementing, or trying to implement, the CFSP in its overseas regions and territories. This chapter aims to see if the EU has been successful in achieving that goal, partly or fully, and if it has strengthen, weaken or had no influence on the integrations between its member states.

---

[43] The Justice and Home Affairs Council is in charge of developing cooperation and common policies on various cross-border issues, with the aim of building an EU-wide area of freedom, security and justice.

Integration and Security Policy

The main lesson of European inner integration is that supranational rules can be reasonably effective even without the traditional state monopoly of coercive power. However, since it is not a state, the union lacks, namely, any military, fiscal, or monetary resources[44] of its own. Its impact rather reflects the normative obligations undertaken by its member states – to accept the straitjacket of double asymmetry, monetary union without fiscal union, and a common security policy without an army. As mentioned in the introduction, the last fact has made France and the UK the dominate states in the shaping of the CFSP throughout the years and they often left Germany – who dominates the shaping of the monetary policy – aside. An important question thus arises: why was Germany not involved in the discussions at St. Malo? This comes down to the belief within the British defence elites at that time (1998), that Germany's armed forces still had many question marks hanging over them, in term of their military capabilities and also their willingness to act. That is to say, it was a British decision not to invite the Germans to St. Malo, and it was not a decision made in any of the EU institutions

But the key country for understanding European integration is not the UK, which is generally against it (as the success of "Brexit" can prove), but rather – the Republic of France. The French led the process of integration with the political field largely free of serious competition, since in the political reality of the post-World War, Germany and Italy could hardly take a lead in the immediate postwar period, while Belgium, Luxembourg, and the Netherlands could not (and still cannot)

---

[44] Not to be confused with policies.

match French economic and military power. This period of French hegemony over the process of European integration during its formative stages had a fundamental consequence for the future shape of European institutions: during that time, ECSC and later the EEC were ideologically led by France, with its very individual tradition of government and conception of civil administration.

A proposed explanation for the French behavior might be that in their perspective, they did not win the Second World War. Furthermore, it is none other than their European rivals – the British, and their overseas rivals – the American, who liberated France from four years of German occupation. France, which was once the strongest power in European politics, whose philosophers influenced the continent's political thinking, whose culture was mimicked by elites across Europe and whose language has been the *Lingua Franca* of diplomacy for centuries, saw its military defeated within six weeks by the German Wehrmacht during the war, and its overseas empire collapsing after the war. The fear of a national rivalry, from the Germans in particular, was phrased cynically by the French novelist, François Mauriac, in the 1950s: "J'aime tellement l'Allemagne que jepréfère qu'il y en ait deux" (I love Germany so much I rather there would be two of them).

France's desire to make Europe's policy, especially its security and defence policy, in its own image, led to France's withdrawal from NATO, after the French President, Charles De Gaulle, protested against the American strong role in the organization and what he perceived as a special relationship between the US and the UK. Without any warning, De Gaulle pulled France out of NATO in 1966, arguing he had to preserve French independence in world affairs. France would have rejoined the organization only forty three years later – in 2009, under President Nicolas Sarkozy. To understand just how influential France had been on military issues from the late 1940s and until the mid-1960s, can be the fact NATO's headquarters was stationed in Paris – not in London Washington. Only after the France withdrew from the alliance, it was relocated in Brussels.

Many in France went beyond this, envisaging a Europe that could challenge American dominance in the field of defence. Already in 1954 a European Defence Community (EDC) was proposed, whose sole purpose was to defend Western Europe from the Soviet threat without the need of American military presence in Europe. The EDC was meant to apply only "in Europe", and not in the overseas regions or territories, yet it failed to come into action. Furthermore, in other EEC member states, the French view of rejecting the American military support was generally resisted. But cooperation in foreign policy evolved to the point where, in the end, it created the CFSP and even the UK, which had long been adamantly opposed to any common action by the EU on defence, joined the initiative of a modest EU defence capacity (in a summit which took place – in France). But this is still a minor element in the union's external relations. The Community's external economic policies remain much more important.

Integration and Foreign Policy

Cooperation in foreign policy among the member states was introduced in 1970 in the form of the EPC as an element of deepening along with the widening to include Britain, Ireland, and Denmark, who joined the EEC in 1973. At that time, the word "political" (the letter P in

EPC) was being used by ministries of foreign affairs, distinguishing what they saw as "high politics" from such matters as economics, evidently regarded as low. But the Community's external economic policies were already a great deal more important than anything the EPC was to achieve during the following years, particularly as France, in the early years after de Gaulle, insisted that the EPC be kept separate from the Community. The EPC did achieve at least one important early result when the member states got human rights placed on the agenda of the Conference on Security and Co-operation in Europe in 1973.[45] The USSR surprisingly accepted the text that was finally adopted; and though nobody then thought this of much consequence, it gave support to the agitation that finally contributed to the dissolution of the Soviet bloc. More generally, the member states' diplomats developed ways of working together that were to produce many joint positions on a wide range of subjects, both in relations with other states and in the United Nations. By 1985 France was ready to accept that the EPC should come closer to the Community and it was included in the Single European Act.

The next formal development of foreign policy cooperation was its incorporation in the TEU, as the "second pillar" of the EU. Article 3(5) of the Treaty states that "in its relations with the wider world, the Union shall uphold and promote its values and interests", implying that the Union exists as a distinct actor in international relations. The prospect of German unification in 1989 had alarmed the French, who feared that the larger Germany would downgrade the Franco-German partnership and

---

[45] The Organization for Security and Co-operation in Europe (OSCE) is the world's largest security-oriented intergovernmental organization. Its mandate includes issues such as arms control and the promotion of human rights, freedom of the press and fair elections.

pursue an autonomous eastern policy. Just as they promoted the single currency to anchor Germany in the EEC, so they wanted a common foreign policy to limit German autonomy in relations with East Asian countries. The Germans, far from opposing this, saw it as part of the design for a Europe united on federal lines just like their own republic.

While the French wanted to strengthen the intergovernmental elements, in particular the European Council, the Germans wanted to move towards a federal system by strengthening the Parliament, so they could hardly speak with one voice about it. The UK under Thatcher wanted neither and, though she accepted the existing EPC, did not want the Community institutions to have a hand in it. While Germany did envisage that foreign policy would move towards becoming a Community competence, France too opposed the idea, and the outcome was the intergovernmental "second pillar" for the CFSP. The CFSP was given a grander name than the EPC and more elaborate institutions. Following Europe's poor showing in the Gulf War, defence was mentioned in the Treaty, but in ambiguous terms to accommodate both the French desire for an autonomous European defence capacity and British opposition to any such thing, for fear it could weaken NATO. So nothing much resulted from the use of the word defence. Nor indeed did the CFSP produce notably better results than the EPC had done before.

European Integration, the CFSP and the Overseas Regions and Territories

From what was written so far, it seems that the CFSP does not really help to strengthen integration within the EU, at least when it comes to policy making within the continent itself. But the internal struggles for power within Europe lasts for centuries, yet the EU's OMRs and OCTs might be the key to increase cohesion of the CFSP and set the EU as a stronger player in international diplomacy. Before the TEU was negotiated in 1991 the relations of the EU (then still the EEC) with its OCTs were the same as with foreign governments, and the OMRs did not play a significant role in the Community's foreign or defensive affairs, and were subjected to their national government. In order to make the overseas regions and territories more valuable to the EEC, the European Development Fund (EDF) was created in 1957 by the *Treaty of Rome* and launched in 1959, targeting mainly the French DOM in order to develop them as if they were "common" regions within the Community. Already in the 1960s, the European Commission tried to establish a regional fund, which would subsequently increase the EEC's influence outside its overseas regions, but only Italy supported it at first. Surprising as it might seem, it was none other but the UK, who backed up the creation of the ERDF before and after its accession in 1973, and the ERDF was eventually created in 1975, under considerable British and Italian pressure.

According to the website of the European Commission, the ERDF aims more than just increase the political and economic influence of the EU through its OMRs and OCTs; it also seeks "to strengthen economic and social cohesion in the European Union by correcting imbalances between its regions". The ERDF is considered as one of the main financial (i.e. "soft power") instruments of the EU's cohesion policy. Its purpose is to contribute to "reducing disparities between the levels of development of European regions and to reduce the backwardness of the least favored regions. Particular attention is to be paid to regions which suffer from severe and permanent natural or demographic handicaps such as the northernmost regions with very low population density as well as island, cross-border and mountain regions." None of the EU sources regarding the ERDF mentions the OMRs or OCTs specifically by their name as the regions with special development challenges. However, as these regions and territories are amongst the poorest of all EU regions, with an average GDP of about 75% of EU's regional average, it is plausible to assume that these regions were one of the main reasons to the British pressure to establish the Fund. One of the interesting benefactors of the ERDF activity, at least in the diplomatic aspect of the CFSP, regards a country which holds no overseas regions, as it had lost all its territories back in 1919 – Germany. The importance of German economy to the funding of the EDF and the ERDF had made it a strong player within the commission, despite its lack of OMRs or OCTs.

European Integration in La Réunion

As mentioned in chapter 1, French policy towards its overseas regions and territories was towards annexation, rather than the British Commonwealth approach. Thus, when it comes to the French OMRs, whether if they're considered DOM or COM for the French themselves, France pushes towards more intervention of EU institutions in the development of its OMRs. As shown on chapter 2, almost all local projects in La Réunion are funded, partly or fully by the ERDF, and although initially this investment is meant to upgrade the island's infrastructure to EU standards, it also uses to promote cooperation of the regional countries with the OMR, and thus increasing the political and economic influence of the EU based on its CFSP.

The EU has been actively involved in the Western Indian Ocean since it launched its counter-piracy operations in 2008, with the help of its Forward Presence Base stationed in La Réunion. Since then, significant financial and human resources have been deployed by EU institutions and member states to enhance maritime security and safety in the region. Promoting a holistic approach to maritime security, it has been investing into training, enhancing national legislation, information-sharing and maritime domain awareness through its Critical Maritime Routes Program (CMR).[46] But the involvement of the EU in the Indian Ocean targets not only the East African countries but the most important country in this region – India. It seems, therefore, that the EU is able to achieve some of its goals, which were put forward in the TEU (Article J.1 of title V) regarding the CFSP, including: the strengthening the security of the Union and its member states in all ways; the preserving peace and strengthen international security; and the promoting of international cooperation. However regarding European integration, the investment in the OMRs has not been much of a success yet.

As mentioned in chapter 2, La Réunion has the second largest population and GDP amongst the OMRs, after the Spanish Canary Islands. It is also the most populated DOM of France, and has twice the GDP of Martinique, which ranked second in the list of French OMRs in terms of GDP. However, excluding Corsica, which is also an island, all France's mainland regions, according to the 2013 division,[47] had a

---

[46] The Critical Maritime Routes program was set up in 2011 and it aims to ensure the security and safety of essential maritime routes.

[47] As of 2016, France has 18 administrative regions, instead of the 27 it had since 1982.

higher GDP, nominal and per capita. For instance, Limousin the region which was ranked one place above La Réunion in the 2013 statistics, had a nominal GDP 6.05% higher than La Réunion's, but since it Limousin has less population, its GDP per capita was 19.19% higher. The same applies to all other French OMRs, though in different figures (mostly much higher).[48] Nevertheless, by examining the growth in GDP in Réunion since 2009, when the TFEU Was due to apply, shows a growth of 5.36% in the years 2009–2013, while in the seven regions ranked above La Réunion in these years, the growth was between 1.87% and 4.66%, which means the massive investment of the EU in the development in the OMRs may lead, by 2020, to them catching up with some of the mainland regions of their national state.

In the past, programs like POSEIDOM for the French DOMs (1989), POSEICAN for the Spanish Canary Islands (1991) and POSEIMA for the Portuguese Azores and Madeira (1991) aimed to improve infrastructure, promote job-creating industries and develop human resources. Since 2004, the EU has had an integrated strategy, based on active partnership between the EU institutions, national governments and the OMRs and in 2006, these programs were replaced by POSEI, with a funding allocation for each of the three EU countries the regions belong to. These actions, alongside the reference to the OMRs needs in the TFEU, means the EU policy makers understand the neglect of the OMRs for five decades and their unique conditions as isolated islands, made them fall behind comparing to the mainland regions of the EU member states'. By correcting this neglect, the EU

---

[48] Martinique had that year a higher GDP per capita than La Réunion, and therefore the difference between it and Limousin was "only" 8.49% if favor for Limousin.

could strengthen the integration between its member states, and initiate further cooperation with geographically distant regions for Europe.

European Integration in the Falkland Islands

While the attitude towards the OMRs, as shown in the case of La Réunion, is of more involvement of EU institutions in the developing of these regions, the case of the OCT is quite the opposite. The EU approach towards the OCTs, as it is expressed in the TFEU, is to give a de-facto more economic and administrative freedom to the OCTs, comparing to the OMRs, as they are not part of the EU and therefore do not comply with its laws and regulations. Though the OCTs also receive funding from the ERDF, these funding are rather new, beginning with the TFEU, and significantly lower than the OMRs. The Falkland Islands, which were used as the case study for the attitude of the EU towards its OCTs, have received a total of €4,130,000 from the ERDF between the years 2013 – 2016. The islands also received an additional aid of €122,518 from the ERDF's technical cooperation facility for technical assistance to draw up the government framework contract. For the years 2014–2020, the ERDF is set to invest a total of €5,900,000 in the islands, which will come to a total of €10,152,518 in seven years. Just for comparison, La Réunion's SEAS-OI project alone, received within the years 2008–2014 a total sum of €10,190,000.

But European integration should not be viewed only by the financial support the EU institutions give to a certain group of islands, but also by how the outside world views the OCTs as part of a larger and stronger political entity. After the publication of the results of the "Brexit" referendum, the government of the Falkland Islands has released an indifferent press statement saying they "will be working across Government, and with the private sector and NGOs, to further investigate all of the potential direct and indirect implications, particularly trade-related, and to ensure that all detail is well documented". The results, however, which favored British leave of the union, might cause a serious concern in the islands. Not only would the Falklands' export market be in danger, because nearly three-quarters of their exports go to the EU market, while they are shut out of most of South America by Argentine pressure, the Islands' sovereignty at risk as well.

Leaving the protective shield of the EU might refuel Argentine aggression towards the islands. Miss Sukey Cameron, the Falkland Islands government representative in the UK, was quoted saying that Britain's secession from the EU "might encourage Argentina to be much more aggressive. The provisions of the *Treaty of Rome* and its successor Treaties, provides the UK and the government of the Falkland Islands with considerable certainty and support from EU member states because of these provisions. Were the UK no longer a member of the EU that support would be much less certain from a large number of those EU member states, and might encourage Argentina to be much more aggressive in its approach". Although European integration is not as visible in the case of the OCTs as it is with the OMRs, through financial EU investments and NGOs involvement, there is still a certain binding between the EU and its OCTs, though officially, these territories are not part of the union.

The unique case of Saint-Martin and Sint Maarten

To add more to the complexity of European integration, the island of Saint Martin in the Caribbean Sea presents and interesting example of the conflict between European centralization and national sovereignty.

On his 1493 voyage, Christopher Columbus spotted the island on the feast day of Saint Martin of Tours[49] (November 11), thus giving the island its name. Though he claimed the island for Spain, Columbus never landed there, and Spain made the settlement of the island low priority. The French and Dutch, on the other hand, did settle in the island which was a center of power struggle for many centuries, as it was a key point of controlling the Caribbean region. Nowadays, the island is controlled by both France (in the northern part) and the Netherlands (in the southern part), with a ratio of 60:40 in favor of the French. At the time this thesis is written, Sint Maarten is still a Dutch overseas territory, and though full independence for the Dutch part is a plausible scenario, the island has a unique status within the EU – it is, at the same time, an OMR (in the Northern part) and an OCT (in the southern part).

As a result of its special status within the EU, the ERDF funds the northern part of the island with special projects, while the southern part is being funded only by the Dutch government. One of these projects was the construction of a public building for the territorial archives, an auditorium and a media library, with the EU donating €3,151,351 (from a total of €9,845,698) in the years 2011–2012. The project consisted of completing a huge piece of infrastructure wholly dedicated to culture

---

[49] Saint Martin of Tours (French: Saint Martin de Tours, d. 397) was Bishop of Tours, whose shrine in France became a famous stopping-point for pilgrims on their road to Santiago de Compostela in Spain.

and the conservation of heritage. The building has three levels, each with an area of approximately 1,600 m^2. It has been designed to host the territorial archives, an auditorium and a media library. The new building has been designed with energy efficiency in mind: there are solar panels on the roof and the frontage includes protective systems to reduce the impact of sunshine and therefore the cost of air conditioning.

Another project funded almost 90% of the total cost by the ERDF, was a language laboratory, for in light of its turbulent history, Saint Martin has inherited many communities speaking different languages: French, English, Spanish, Dutch, Creole, etc. This uniqueness, and its focus on tourism, meant that multilingualism is a necessity on the island of Saint Martin. Language learning, as part of secondary and higher education, is therefore a key element in education policy. In order to carry out this training successfully, a language laboratory was necessary. However, due to the island nature and small size of the community it lacks of teachers, particularly for higher-level education requiring specialist skills. It was therefore necessary for the laboratory to have an effective connection to the rest of the world, to allow students to find their teachers wherever they are.

The project's goal was to install a language laboratory equipped with high-performance information and communication technology equipment. It involves setting up and putting into operation a multimedia space dedicated to language learning: 30 work stations (including two accessible to disabled people), an interactive white-board, two cameras, two video projectors, priority Internet access and, of course, all the learning software in the language laboratory. The intense investment of the ERDF in a language laboratory is quite understandable: with more than twenty official languages recognized by the Union, interpersonal communication throughout the EU is a big challenge for European integration, and both the public library and the language laboratory in Saint Martin, can help the EU strengthen the communication among its citizens, as it has no central language of its own.

Map of Saint Martin and its division

The Future of European Integration after "Brexit"

With the expected secession of the UK from the EU, France would become the union's member state with the most overseas regions and territories. The question which might rise is: will the British secession necessarily harm European integration, leaving France as the dominant military and diplomatic power of the Union? It is hard to give an unambiguous answer for that. Facing the new reality in European politics, Germany and France have outlined plans to deepen European military cooperation, as Britain's exit from the Union removes one of the biggest obstacles to stronger EU defence in tandem with NATO. In potentially the biggest leap in European defence since the 1990s, the German and the French are laying out ways for the bloc to rapidly deploy forces, with security cooperation emerging as a unifying force for Europe after Britain's vote to leave.

The decision to relaunch closer military cooperation, which was first tried by Britain and France in 1998, goes beyond Britain's decision to leave the EU, according to some diplomats who are involved in the new plan. No European nation has the resources alone to confront failing states on Europe's borders, Islamist militants or a resurgent Russia. This cooperation between the German and the French should not come as a surprise, as support in these countries to a stronger integration on European level, even in defence issues, is stronger than the EU average. In fact, in all six founding member states of the EEC the support for stronger integration on the EU level, in all aspects, and this includes a defence policy.

Among the "founding six", support of EU decision making on foreign affairs issues is between 66% (Luxemburg) and 81% (Belgium), with an average of 72.1% which is 6.7% higher from the EU average; on defence, however, issues the support is between 56% (Luxemburg) and 72% (Belgium), with an average of 62.3% but that is still 27.4% higher from the EU average (which is below 49%). These statistics might show that Britain's secession of the EU will not cause it to fall apart and weaken its inner integration, but quite the contrary – it would strengthen it. Losing one of the most important pillar states of the union, especially in the military aspect, is a warning sign to the EU decision makers that integration is not strong enough yet, and new methods should be reviewed on how to improve integration among the EU member states.

Chapter Summary

One of the main ideas behind the CFSP was to strengthen the European integration among the EU member states. Several attempts have been made at conceptualizing the EU's CFSP. A first generation of scholars, focusing on the coherence of policies, discussed the extent to which the EU might be referred to as a foreign policy actor. The argument about the EU's foreign policy and security policy circles the question into which extend should the EU be involved in the member states' policy making in these fields, with the neighboring countries of the EU and overseas. The assumption is the more power held by EU institutions when it comes to foreign and security policies, the stronger the bond between its member states. Thus, if the EU is responsible of the foreign and security policies of its member states, it also responsible to apply them in their overseas regions and territories, a field the EU (and its preexisting form – the EEC) was trying to avoid for decades.

The feeling that the union should provide more effective military backing for its common policy in former Yugoslavia (during the Balkan wars) spurred governments to strengthen its capacity in the field of defence. While all recognize that they depend on NATO for defence against any major threat to their security, they used somewhat stronger language in the *Treaty of Amsterdam* than in the TEU, envisaging "the progressive framing of a common defence policy, which might lead to a common defence". The war over Kosovo (1998–1999) demonstrated that the European countries were capable of delivering only one-tenth of the firepower, and their influence over the conduct of the action was correspondingly limited. This brought together the British and French to launch their defence initiative in St. Malo.

The experiences in the Gulf (1991) and the Balkan wars had shown the French that they had to come closer to NATO if they were to make an effective military contribution. The British for their part had come to see the merit of working with the French, and the British government saw defence as a field in which a central role for Britain in the union could be secured. But European integration had also its failures regarding the CFSP. Though in 2001 the NATO member states of the EU joined the US in its war in Afghanistan, as part of the "War on Terror" the American president, George W. Bush, has declared as a consequence of the September 11 attacks, the situation in the Iraq War was different. Of the "leading trio" of the EU (France, Germany and the UK), only the British had supported the American offensive in Iraq, making it impossible for the EU to sustain a coherent and common foreign policy or security policy, as the French and the German strongly opposed the US invasion of Iraq.

The European integration in the overseas regions and territories seems to be influenced from the integration on state level, and from public opinion within the Union. Thus, the integration in the regions which are part of the EU (the OMRs) is stronger than in territories which are not part of the Union, like the Falkland Islands. In addition, it seems that integration in foreign policy, which receives more support of public opinion, is stronger than the integration in security policy, which many EU citizens still see as a matter of the nation states. Nevertheless, the expected secession of the UK from the union and the increasing cooperation between France and Germany in the field of common security might strengthen the integration of the EU member states in the mainland and in the overseas regions (OMRs) at least.

SUMMARY

The Common Foreign and Security Policy of the EU, introduced in Maastricht in 1992, was another milestone in the strengthening of integration of the small European community which was established in the 1950s – the European Economic Community. Within forty-five years, the community doubled the number if its members (from six to twelve) but what held these member states together was not only the economic cooperation – it was also the Soviet threat, which had ended 1989, leaving a "void" in a search of a common "other" which helped shape the new European identity. In order to analyze the European Union properly, it is important to understand the historical context behind it. The EEC was created in the context of the Cold War. The Cold War was "born" in the context of the aftermath of the Second World War. The Second World War erupted as a result of the history of Europe. Just as the name of La Réunion was an outcome of European history, the same applies on the dispute between Argentina and the UK over the Falkland Islands, and the odd division of the island of Saint Martin.

This research has presented the EU comprehensive **approach**, as it showed what the EU is aiming to achieve through its actions, rather than the EU comprehensive **policy**, which deals with what the EU actually does. The goal of European cohesion is that both approach and policy will coincide, in order to reach greater integration.

Conclusions

The end of the Second World War also brought to an end most of the remaining overseas colonial empires of Europe. In some cases, the struggle was peaceful, in others – violent. One of the reasons the European colonial powers decided to give up their colonies in Asia, Africa and South America during the 1950s, 1960s and 1970s, was that they believed this action could lower the need to defend these territories by the "mother state", while creating new states which will support the Euro-American efforts in the Cold War against the Soviet Bloc. This policy gained only partial success, as most of these new countries chose to join the Non-Aligned Movement, and some even sided with the USSR. Nevertheless, the European former colonial powers, especially Britain and France, left some overseas territories as national assents, either as part of their empire (the UK) or as an assimilated regions overseas (France). However, in the early days of the EEC, neither the community nor the states themselves knew what role will these dominions play, and the fact the French were willing to lease French Guiana to the Israelis, only proves that in the first decades of the community, the full potential of these dominions was not discovered.

Nonetheless, with the years passing, the OMRs and OCTs became much more valuable to the EEC and later to the EU in terms of research (the European Space Agency), maritime security and integration (the Falkland War) and also diplomacy. The process which started in 1997 in Amsterdam, with the distinct definition of these dominions, ended in 2007 in Lisbon with much clearer role to each region and territory, extracting much of their potential to the benefit of the OMRs and OCTs, the EU and neighboring countries.

With the increasing importance of the OMRs in the view of the policy makers in Brussels, new project, funded by European related-to-mission funds (such as the EFF, EAFRD and POSEI) were established in all the OMRs, in accordance to their population, terrain, location and international cooperation. The French DOM, La Réunion, was selected as a case study due to its size (in means of population) and its diplomatic importance to the EU, in means of international cooperation in the Indian Ocean region. The projects which are placed in La Réunion demonstrate how the EU uses its "soft power" instruments to increase its influence in remote parts of the world. However the influence of the "parent state" and previous colonial condition of some countries in the region are still visible. The fact that the official website of the Indian Ocean Commission is yet solely in French, gives evidence that the EU has still plenty of work to be done, in order to make cooperation in a broader scale.

Nevertheless, the bottom line is – the foreign policy implemented by the EU in its OMRs has proven itself successful, both for external relations and internal integration. Without the EU projects in its OMRs, the influence of the EU outside its immediate "neighborhood" would be much smaller, as it would likely not have the public's justification for such investment in remote projects. In addition, since the EU is now involved in the development of the OMRs, and not just the "mother state", the policies determined in Brussels, regarding foreign relations in remote regions are more coherent (though still need some improvement, as the case of the Indian Ocean Commission proves).

It seems to me, based on the case study of La Réunion, that although the importance of France in the development of the region is still strongly visible, it is hard to ignore the long way the EU has passed since the 1950s. Back then, the development of the OMRs was dependent completely on the "mother state". Today, the EU has reached a level of internal cooperation where there are joint projects in these regions, funded by the EU, and which are beneficial to the neighboring countries as well, thus increasing the EU's importance overseas. Another important aspect in the EU's growing influence overseas is that it is based strongly on **civilian** projects ("soft power") rather than **military** presence ("hard power"). This fact corresponds with the EU's ambitions to be an organization which promotes peace, not violence.

Although the EU promotes itself as an organization which prefers diplomacy over violent force, the importance of a common security policy cannot be neglected, both for internal and external reasons. The end of the Cold War in 1989 marked a new era in Europe. The common enemy was gone, and the need for NATO's assistance in defending the continent from an external invasion was eliminated. Nevertheless, in order to increase the internal integration within the EU, the member states had to start "talking" in a single and coherent voice, thus the CFSP was presented in 1992. Furthermore, due to its OMRs and OCTs, the EU is a maritime power, whether the policy makers in Brussels are aware of it or not. At the time when this thesis is being written, the UK is still part of the union, and so are its many overseas military bases. Even so, after Britain's departure of the EU, it would still have France's, Portugal's and Spain's islands around the world, which would keep it as a strategic player in the world's international maritime trade, and it would have to protect them. The case of the Falkland War shows just how delicate is the CSDP is, since there are two obstacles in the way: (1) Some states, like the UK, prefer to take care security issues on their own, requesting only diplomatic support when needed, and (2) some member states of the EU, especially those who did not take part in any military conflict since 1945, don't appreciate any use of force against another country, as the case of the sinking of the Argentine Cruiser General Belgrano, and the death of its 300 sailors, indicates.

In chapter 3 I mentioned that the EU sees security as the first condition for development. My assumption is, based on this statement, published in an official EU document, that it is the EU's belief that through peace and cooperation, wrapped in an atmosphere of personal safety and national security, the EU could help its own member states, as well as to third world country, develop a better future for humanity. By providing this kind of security, using of the EU's OMRs and OCTs, the union can plan ahead (as it did with the *Territorial Agenda of the European Union 2020* and the *Europe 2020 Strategy*) and build it maritime presence around the world, to provide security for international trade both to and from the EU.

Since The CSDP gives a general guideline of action of the EU during a time of crisis, it can also help loosen the EU's rely on the NATO. This dependence is getting rather problematic, especially since the election of Donald Trump put to question the possibility of an American aid to Europe in case of a major military operation. By building its naval capabilities, based on internal cooperation, the EU can increase the integration among its member states to other fields in security and defence as well, a sensitive subjects in many states within the union nowadays.

The CFSP is aimed to achieve not only better results for the EU as far as foreign policy and security and defence policy are concerned, but it also has an important role in increasing integration within the EU. Since the union lacks any military, fiscal, or monetary resources of its own, the common policies it initiates, are served to overcome this obstacle. However, as long as the UK is part of the union, it seems the EU resembles a three-headed hydra when it comes to the CFSP: France, who wishes to strengthen the status of the overseas regions and territories; Britain, who wishes to limit it as much as possible; and Germany, who does not see the overseas issues as a priority for the union as a whole. Nevertheless, through financial and strategic investment in the OMRs and OCTs in the twenty years which has passed since the *Treaty of Amsterdam*, the importance and influence of these dominions on the CFSP, at least outside the European "neighborhood", has increased, as it was shown in this thesis so far.

The EU has a declared agenda regarding it maritime strategy, which is not done on a state level anymore (as it was in St. Malo in 1998), but on an EU level, corresponding with all the member states of the union, even if they have no overseas regions or territories of their own. As it was explained in the last chapter of this thesis, "Brexit" may have a POSITIVE effect on EU integration, both inland and overseas, as one of the greatest opposers for an increasing integration on the CFSP level – the UK – will no longer have a "say" in this matter.

In my opinion, if France and Germany, the two most important countries of the union regarding military power and diplomacy respectively, would join forces and lead (rather than dictate) the course towards greater integration in the EU, while not neglecting the union's citizens living outside Europe, it will be to the benefit of all.

BIBLIOGRAPHY

Primary Sources

Commission de l'Océan Indien. *Union Européenne – COI: Ensemble Pour le Développement Durable et Solidaire de l'Indianocéanie*, 2016.

Council of the European Union. *European Security Strategy: A Secure Europe in a Better World*. Brussels: European Communities, 2009.

Council of the European Union, *Maritime Security Strategy*, 2014.

European Commission. *Europe 2020: A European Strategy for Smart, Sustainable and Inclusive Growth*. Brussels: European Commission, 2010.

European Commission, *Progress of the EU's Integrated Maritime Policy*, 2012.

European Commission. *The EU's Comprehensive Approach to External Conflict and Crises*, 2013.

European Commission, *The Outermost Regions: European Regions of Assets and Opportunities*, 2012.

European Communities. *Treaty of Amsterdam Amending the Treaty on European Union, the Treaties Establishing the European Communities and Certain Related Acts*. Luxembourg: Office for Official Publications of the European Communities, 1997.

European Parliament, *Regulation (EU) No 1301/2013 of the European Parliament and of the Council*, 2013.

European Parliament. *The Status and Location of the Military Installations of the Member States of the European Union and Their Potential Role for the European Security and Defence Policy (ESDP)*, 2009.

European Union. *European Perspective on Specific Types of Territories*, 2012.

European Union. *Growth Factors in the Outermost Regions*, 2011.

European Union. *Territorial Agenda of the European Union 2020: Towards an Inclusive, Smart and Sustainable Europe of Diverse Regions*, 2011.

Academic Sources

Adaoğlu, Hacer Soykan. "Special Territories in European Union and North Cyprus: A Sui Generis Relationship Under Community Law." *Uluslararası İlişkiler* 23 (2009): 127 – 148.

Agné, Hans. "Irretrievable Powers and Democratic Accountability." In *The Illusion of Accountability in the European Union*, edited by Sverker Gustavsson, Christer Karlsson and Thomas Persson, 51 – 66. New York: Routledge, 2009.

Allen, Richard B. *Slaves, Freedmen and Indentured Laborers in Colonial Mauritius*. Cambridge: Cambridge University Press, 1999.

Amtenbrink, Fabian. "EMU and the Overseas." In *EU Law of the Overseas*, edited by Dimitry Kochenov, 271 – 290. Biggleswade: Kluwer Law International, 2011.

Aimaq, Jasmine. *For Europe or Empire?*. Lund: Lund University Press, 1996.

Beit-Hallahmi, Benjamin. *The Israeli Connection: Whom Israel Arms and Why*. London: I.B. Tauris & Co, 1987.

Benson, Timothy. "Suez 1956." *History Today* 56 (2006).Accessed June 15, 2016. http://www.historytoday.com/timothy-benson/suez-1956.

Blockmans, Steven. "Between the Devil and the Deep Blue Sea? Conflicts in External Action Pursued by OCTs and the EU." In *EU Law of the Overseas*, In EU Law of the Overseas, edited by Dimitry Kochenov, 307 – 321. Biggleswade: Kluwer Law International, 2011.

Bonde, Jens-Peter. *Consolidated Reader-Friendly Edition of the Treaty on European Union (TEU) and the Treaty on the Functioning of the European Union (TFEU) as amended by the Treaty of Lisbon (2007)*. Notat Grafisk: Foundation for EU Democracy, 2008.

Buruma, Ian. *Year Zero: A History of 1945*. New York: The Penguin Press, 2013.

Chamberlain, Muriel E. *The Longest Companion to European Decolonisation in the Twentieth Century*. London: Longman, 1998.

Cohen, Elie. "The Euro, Economic Federalism, and the Question of National Sovereignty." In *The Idea of Europe from Antiquity to the European Union*, edited by Anthony Pagden, 260 – 287. Cambridge: Cambridge University Press, 2002.

Collier, David. "The Comparative Method." In *Political Science: The State of the Discipline II*, edited by Ada W. Finifter, 105 – 119. Washington, DC: American Political Science Association, 1993.

Cooper, Fredrick. "Reconstructing Empire in British and French Africa." *Past and Present* 210 (2011): 196 – 120.

Corbett, Julian S. *Some Principles of Maritime Strategy*. New York: Longmans, Green and Co., 1918.

Custos, Dominique. "Implications of the European Integration for the Overseas." In *EU Law of the Overseas*, edited by Dimitry Kochenov, 91 – 120. Biggleswade: Kluwer Law International, 2011.

Dühr, Stefanie, Dominic Stead and Wil Zonneveld. "The Europeanization of Spatial Planning Through Territorial Cooperation." *Planning Practice & Research* 22, no. 3 (2007): 291 – 307.

Edwards, Geoffrey. "Europe and the Falkland Islands Crisis 1982." *Journal of Common Market Studies* 22 (1984): 295 – 313.

Foa, Bruno. "Europe in Ruins." In *Sources of European History Since 1900*, edited by Marvin Perry, Matthew Berg and James Krukones, 275 – 277. Boston, Wadsworth, 2011.

Frémeaux, Jacques. "France: Empire and the Mère-Patrie." In *The Age of Empires*, edited by Robert Aldrich, 152 – 175. London: Thames & Hudson Ltd., 2007.

Gad, Ulrik Pram and Adler-Nissen, Rebecca. "Introduction: Postcolonial Sovereignty Games." In European *Integration and Postcolonial Sovereignty Games*, edited by Rebecca Adler-Nissen and Ulrik Pram Gad, 1 – 24. New York: Routledge, 2013.

George, Alexander L. and Bennett, Andrew. *Case Studies and Theory Development in the Social Sciences*. Cambridge: MIT Press, 2005.

George, Stephen. *An Awkward Partner: Britain in the European Community*. Oxford: Oxford University Press, 1990.

Gibran, Daniel. *The Falklands War: Britain Versus the Past in the South Atlantic*. Jefferson: McFarland & Company, Inc, 1998.

Gillingham, John. *European Integration, 1950 – 2005: Superstate or New Market Economy?*. Cambridge: Cambridge University Press, 2003.

Hast, Susanna. *Spheres of Influence in International Relations*. New York: Routledge, 2014.

Hintjens, Helen and Hodge, Dorothea. "The UK Caribbean Overseas Territories: Governing Unruliness Amidst the Extra-Territorial EU." *Commonwealth & Comparative Politics* 50 (2012): 190 – 225.

Hitchcock, William I. *The Struggle for Europe*. New York: Anchor Books, 2004.

Keohane, Daniel. "ESDP and NATO." In *European Security and Defence Policy: The First 10 Years*, edited by. Giovanni Grevi, Damien Helly and Daniel Keohane, 127 – 138. Paris: The European Union Institute for Security Studies, 2009.

Kochenov, Dimitry. "The Application of EU Law in the EU's Overseas Regions, Countries, and Territories After the Entry Into Force of the Treaty of Lisbon." *Michigan State International Law Review* 20 (2013): 669 – 743.

Kochenov, Dimitry. "The EU and the Overseas: Outermost Regions, Associated Overseas Countries and Territories with the Union, and Territories Sui Generis." In *EU Law of the Overseas*, edited by Dimitry Kochenov, 3 – 67. Biggleswade: Kluwer Law International, 2011.

Kochenov, Dimitry. "EU Citizenship in the Overseas." In *EU Law of the Overseas*, edited by Dimitry Kochenov, 199 – 220. Biggleswade: Kluwer Law International, 2011.

Kyle, Keith. *Suez: Britain's End of Empire in the Middle East*. London: I.B. Tauris, 2011.

Lauren, Paul Gordon. *The Evolution of International Human Rights: Visions Seen*. Philadelphia: University of Pennsylvania Press, 2011.

Lind, Michael. "Toward a Global Society of States." *The Wilson Quarterly* 26 (2002): 59 – 69.

Lőrincz, András. "The Importance of the Outermost Regions for Strengthening EU Foreign and Regional Relations." *Paper presented at the International Conference on The EU as a Global Actor*, Berlin, July 7 – 10, 2011.

Louis, William Roger. "American Anti-Colonialism and the Dissolution of the British Empire." *International Affairs* 61, no. 2 (1985): 395 – 420.

Major, Claudia and Mölling, Christian. "EU Military Capabilities – Some European Troops, but not yet a European Army." In *EU Crisis Management: Institutions and Capabilities in the Making*, edited by Ettore Greco, Nicoletta Pirozzi and Stefano Silvestri, 11 – 28. Rome: Istituto Affari Internazionali, 2010.

Marshall, Peter J. "British Imperial Territories from 1783." In *The Cambridge Illustrated History of the British Empire*, edited by Peter J. Marshall, 384 – 388. Cambridge: Cambridge University Press, 1996.

Marshall, Peter J. "Introduction: The World Shaped by Empire." In *The Cambridge Illustrated History of the British Empire*, edited by Peter J. Marshall, 147 – 184.Cambridge: Cambridge University Press, 1996.

Marseille, Jacques. *Empire Colonial et Capitalisme Français*. Paris: Éditions Albin Michel, 1984.

Martin, Lisa L. "Institutions and Cooperation: Sanctions during the Falkland Islands Conflict." *International Security* 16 (1992): 143 – 178.

Martinez, Ian. "Spain's "Splendid Little War" with Morocco." *The International Lawyer* 37 (2003): 871 – 881.

Mayall, James. "The Shadow of Empire: The EU and the Former Colonial World." In *International Relations and the European Union*, edited by Christopher Hill and Michael Smith, 292 – 316. Oxford: Oxford University Press, 2005.

McKenzie, Kirsten. "Britain: Ruling the Waves." In *The Age of Empires*, edited by Robert Aldrich, 128 – 151. London: Thames & Hudson Ltd., 2007.

McDowell, Robert M. "Falkland Islands Biogeography: Converging Trajectories in the South Atlantic Ocean." *Journal of Biogeography* 32 (2005): 49 – 62.

Mira, Pedro Solbes. *Europe's Outermost Regions and the Single Market: The EU's Influence in the World*. Brussels: European Commission, 2011.

Miskimmon, Alister. *Germany and the Common Foreign and Security Policy of the European Union*. London: Palgrave Macmillan, 2007.

Mix, Derek E. *The European Union: Foreign and Security Policy*. Washington: Congressional Research Service, 2013.

Moriarty, Henry Augustus. *Islands in the Southern Indian Ocean Westward of Longitude 80 Degrees East, Including Madagascar*. London: Great Britain Hydrographic Office, 1891.

Muller, Karis. "Europe as a Pacific Power." In *EU Law of the Overseas*, edited by Dimitry Kochenov, 341 – 361. Biggleswade, Kluwer Law International, 2011.

Murray, Fiona. *The European Union and Member States Territories: A New Legal Framework under the EU Treaties*. The Hague: Asser Press, 2012.

Nasson, Bill. *Britain's Empire: Making a British World*. Stroud: Tempus Publishing Limited, 2004.

Pejsova, Eva. *Scrambling for the Indian Ocean*. Paris: European Union Institute for Security Studies, 2016.

Peters, Dirk. "European Security Policy for the People? Public Opinion and the EU's Common Foreign, Security and Defence Policy." *European Security* 23 (2014): 388 – 408.

Pinder, John. *The European Union: A Very Short Introduction*. Oxford: Oxford University Press, 2001.

Pollard, Sidney. "Shipping and the British Economy since 1870: A Retrospective View." In *Exploiting the Sea: Aspects of Britain's Maritime Economy since 1870*, edited by David J. Starkey and Alan G. Jamieson, 93 – 103. Exeter: University of Exeter Press, 1998.

Riddick, John F. *The History of British India: A Chronology*. Westport: Praeger, 2006.

Roberts, John M. *The Penguin History of Europe*. London: Penguin Books, 1997.

Ruttley, Philip. "The Long Road to Unity: The Contribution of Law to the Process of European Integration since 1945." In *The Idea of Europe from Antiquity to the European Union*, edited by Anthony Pagden, 228 – 259. Cambridge: Cambridge University Press, 2002.

Salomon, Markus. "Recent European Initiatives in Marine Protection Policy: Towards Lasting Protection for Europe's Seas?." *Environmental Science & Policy* 12 (2009): 359 – 366.

Selosse, Sandrine, Olivia Ricci, Sabine Garabedian, and Nadia Maizi. *Reunion Island Energy Autonomy Objective by 2030*. St-Denis: Université de la Réunion, 2014.

Shaelou, Stéphanie Laulhé. "The Principle of Territorial Exclusion in the EU: SBAs in Cyprus – a Special Case of Sui Generis Territories in the EU." In *EU Law of the Overseas*, ed. Dimitry Kochenov, 153 – 175. Biggleswade: Kluwer Law International, 2011.

Shipway, Martin. *Decolonization and Its Impact – A Comparative Approach to the End of the Colonial Empires*. Malden: Blackwell, 2008.

Sjursen, Helene. "The EU's Common Foreign and Security Policy: The Quest for Democracy." *Journal of European Public Policy* 18 (2011): 1069 – 1077.

Smith, Karen E. "The Outsiders: The European Neighbourhood Policy." *International Affairs* 81 (2005): 757 – 773.

Stockwell, Anthony J. "Suez and the Moral Bankruptcy of Empire." *History Today* 56 (2006).Accessed June 15, 2016. http://www.historytoday.com/aj-stockwell/suez-and-moral-bankruptcy-empire.

Stockwell, Anthony J. "Power, Authority and Freedom." In *The Cambridge Illustrated History of the British Empire*, edited by Peter J. Marshall, 147 – 184. Cambridge: Cambridge University Press, 1996.

Strang, David. "Global patterns of decolonization, 1500 – 1987." *International Studies Quarterly* 35 (1991): 429 – 454.

Sutton, Paul. "The European Union and the Caribbean Region: Situating the Caribbean Overseas Countries and Territories." *European Review of Latin American and Caribbean Studies* 93 (2012): 79 – 94.

Trybus, Martin. "The Vision of the European Defence Community and a Common Defence for the European Union." In *European Security Law*, edited by Martin Trybus, 13 – 42. Oxford: Oxford University Press, 2007.

Urwin, Derek W. *The Community of Europe: A History of European Integration since 1945*. New York: Routledge, 2014.

Van Vooren, Bart. "The European Union as an International Actor and Progressive Experimentation in its Neighborhood." In *European Foreign Policy*, edited by Panos Koutrakos, 147 – 171. Cheltenham: Edward Elgar, 2011.

Vaxellaire, Daniel. *Le Grand Livre de l'Histoire de La Réunion, vol. 1: Des Origines à 1848*. Saint-Denis: Éditions Orphie, 2003.

Vaxellaire, Daniel. *Le Grand Livre de l'Histoire de La Réunion, vol. 2: De 1848 à Nos Jours*. Saint-Denis: Éditions Orphie, 2003.

Vego, Milan. *Maritime Strategy and Sea control: Theory and Practice*. New York: Routledge, 2016.

Vestergaard, Cindy. "The European Union, its Overseas Territories and Non-Proliferation: The Case of Arctic Yellowcake." *EU Non-Proliferation Consortium* 25 (2013): 1 – 11.

Webber, Mark, Stuart Croft, Jolyon Howorth, Terry Terriff, and Elke Krahmann. "The Governance of European Security." *Review of International Studies* 30 (2004): 3 – 26.

Ziller, Jacques. "The European Union and the Territorial Scope of European Territories." *Victoria University of Wellington Law Review* 38 (2007): 51 – 64.

Internet Sources

Baczynska, Gabriela and Emmott, Robin. "Germany, France Seek Stronger EU Defence after Brexit: Document." *Reuters*, September 12, 2016. Accessed October 19, 2016. http://www.reuters.com/article/us-europe-defence-idUSKCN11I1XU.

Centre Virtuel de la Connaissance sur l'Europe. "Decolonisation in Asia." Decolonisation: Geopolitical Issues and Impact. Last modified June 13, 2016. http://www.cvce.eu/en/education/unit-content/-/unit/dd10d6bf-e14d-40b5-9ee6-37f978c87a01/185a58dc-2a7e-43d3-bf54-8e4a25a9964f.

Cody, Edward. "After 43 Years, France to Rejoin NATO as Full Member." *The Washington Post*, March 12, 2009. Accessed October 1, 2016. http://www.washingtonpost.com/wp-dyn/content/article/2009/03/11/AR2009031100547.html.

Commission de l'Océan Indien. "Les missions de la COI." Indianocéanie, un avenir à bâtir ensemble. Last modified September 6, 2016. http://commissionoceanindien.org/a-propos/qui-sommes-nous/.

European Commission. "European Regional Development Fund." Regional Policy. Last modified October 6, 2016. http://ec.europa.eu/regional_policy/EN/funding/erdf/.

European Commission. "Falkland Islands." Overview. Last modified October 19, 2016. http://ec.europa.eu/europeaid/countries/falkland-islands_en.

European Commission. "One of EU's Outermost Regions Receiving Transport Boost." Regional Policy. Last modified September 6, 2016. http://ec.europa.eu/regional_policy/en/projects/france/one-of-eus-outermost-regions-receiving-transport-boost.

European Commission. "Réunion's New Wastewater System Fully Complies with EU Standards." Regional Policy. Last modified September 6, 2016. http://ec.europa.eu/regional_policy/en/projects/france/reunions-new-wastewater-system-fully-complies-with-eu-standards.

European Union. "About CSDP – Overview." European Union External Action. Last modified September 15, 2016. http://www.eeas.europa.eu/csdp/about-csdp/index_en.htm.

European Union. "Common Foreign and Security Policy (CFSP)."Security and Defence. Last modified September 15, 2016. http://eeas.europa.eu/topics/common-foreign-security-policy-cfsp/420/common-foreign-and-security-policy-cfsp_en.

European Union. "European Neighbourhood Policy (ENP)." European External Action Service. Last modified September 4, 2016. http://eeas.europa.eu/enp/about-us/index_en.htm.

European Union. "Indian Ocean Commission." Regional Integration. Last modified September 6, 2016. http://eeas.europa.eu/delegations/mauritius/regional_integration/indian_ocean_commission/index_en.htm.

Falkland Islands Government. "EU Referendum 2016." Press Releases. Last modified October 19, 2016. http://www.falklands.gov.fk/eu-referendum-2016/.

Falkland Islands Government. "Our History." Our People. Last modified September 11, 2016. http://www.falklands.gov.fk/our-people/our-history/.

Falkland Islands Government. "Our Islands, Our History." Our People. Last modified September 19, 2016. http://www.falklands.gov.fk/assets/OurIslandsOurHistory1.pdf.

Faye, Olivier. "Hollande va « adapter » le Pacte de Responsabilité à la Réunion." Le Monde, August 21, 2010. Accessed September 6, 2016. http://www.lemonde.fr/politique/article/2014/08/21/les-annonces-de-hollande-pour-la-reunion_4474489_823448.html.

Hague, William. "Leaving the EU Would be Disastrous for the Falklands, Gibraltar and Ulster." The Telegraph, May 9, 2016. Accessed October 19, 2016. http://www.telegraph.co.uk/news/2016/05/09/leaving-the-eu-would-be-disastrous-for-the-falklands-gibraltar-a/.

Hellenic Resource Network. "Title V: Provisions on a Common Foreign and Security Policy." Documents. Last modified October 6, 2016. http://www.hri.org/docs/Maastricht92/mt_title5.html.

Institut National de la Statistique et des Études Économiques. "Produits Intérieurs Bruts Régionaux et Valeurs Ajoutées Régionales de 1990 à 2013." Statistiques. Last modified October 6, 2016. http://www.insee.fr/fr/themes/detail.asp?reg_id=99&ref_id=pib-va-reg-base-2010.

Le Blog de JP Guillerot. "La Réunion de 1945 à Nos Jours." Cours et conseils en histoire géo au lycée. Last modified September 2, 2016. http://jpguillerot.over-blog.fr/article-26969342.html.

Le Monde Diplomatique. "Allemagne, Histoire d'une Ambition." Manière de Voir. Last modified October 1, 2016. http://www.monde-diplomatique.fr/mav/116/.

Macias, Amanda Jeremy Bender, and Skye Gould. "The 35 Most Powerful Militaries in the World." Business Insider, December 10, 2014. Accessed September 11, 2016. http://www.businessinsider.com/the-worlds-most-powerful-militaries-2014-12.

Miller, Lewis G. "Brussels, Britain and the Falklands War." The Strix, May 1, 2016. Accessed September 11, 2016. http://www.thestrix.com/britains-eu-membership-and-the-falklands-war/.

NATO." The Atlantic Charter." NATO Official Texts. Last modified June 5, 2016. http://www.nato.int/cps/en/natohq/official_texts_16912.htm

One Europe. "EU Overseas Countries and Territories and Outermost Regions." European Overseas Territories. Last modified June 30, 2016. http://one-europe.info/eurographics/eu-overseas-countries-and-territories-and-outermost-regions.

Riley-Smith, Ben. "Leaving EU Would Fuel Argentine Aggression towards Falkland Islands, Official Claims." The Telegraph, April 26, 2016. Accessed October 19, 2016. http://www.telegraph.co.uk/news/2016/04/25/leaving-eu-would-fuel-argentinian-aggression-towards-falkland-is/.

Stephens, Bret. "Why the Falklands Matter." The Wall Street Journal, April 9, 2012. Last modified September 21, 2016. http://www.wsj.com/articles/SB10001424052702303815404577333520361035492.

The Daily Herald. "Call for Completion of Independence Trajectory." The Daily Herald, October 14, 2016. Accessed October 19, 2016. https://thedailyherald.sx/islands/60933-call-for-completion-of-independence-trajectory.

Université Blaise Pascal. "Survey of Environment Assisted by Satellite in the Indian Ocean." SEAS OI. Last modified September 6, 2016. ftp://ftpobs.univ-bpclermont.fr/GEOL/volcano/druitt_esf/4437%20Harris/Presentations/130529_theme4_talk4_Catry.pdf.

Wikipedia. "Falklands War." Falklands War. Last modified September 20, 2016. https://en.wikipedia.org/wiki/Falklands_War.

World atlas. "Saint Martin." Description. Last modified October 19, 2016. http://www.worldatlas.com/webimage/countrys/namerica/caribb/stmartin.htm.

World atlas. "Saint Martin Large Color Map." Description. Last modified October 19, 2016. http://www.worldatlas.com/webimage/countrys/namerica/caribb/lgcolor/stmartin.htm.